"THE LIBRARY MANAGER'S GUIDE TO AUTOMATION"

2ND EDITION

BY

RICHARD W. BOSS

Knowledge Industry Publications, Inc.
White Plains, NY and London

Professional Librarian Series

The Library Manager's Guide to Automation, 2nd Edition

Library of Congress Cataloging in Publication Data

Boss, Richard W.
    The library manager's guide to automation.

    Bibliography: p.
    Includes index.
    1. Libraries—Automation.   I. Title.
Z678.9.B66   1983   025'.02'02854   83-19886
ISBN 0-86729-052-8
ISBN 0-86729-051-x (pbk.)

Printed in the United States of America

10   9   8   7   6   5   4   3   2   1

Table of Contents

List of Figures and Tables

1

Introduction

The crisis facing libraries that was described in the first edition of *The Library Manager's Guide to Automation** continues. The crisis consists of a combination of elements: the "information explosion," the appearance of an increasing amount of information in nonprint formats, changing expectations of library users and the loss of authority by library managers. Additional factors are increasing costs for library materials, personnel, and construction materials and labor for building new libraries.

As we approach the mid-1980s, more information is being generated than ever before. Regardless of the state of the economies, the publishing output of the nations of the world increases by at least 5% per year. Paul E. Peters has described the phenomenon as it affects libraries as a "publication explosion" because its impact is "always stated in terms of journal titles, journal articles, technical reports and the like."[1]

Each year an increasing amount of information becomes available online, on magnetic tape, on video disc or in some other format not commonly held by libraries. Initially, the publications in these formats had print counterparts, but more and more original publishing is being done solely in nonprint form. Therefore, it is essential that libraries accommodate the new formats by purchasing equipment and acquiring new expertise.

The cost of the publications bought by libraries has been rising much faster than the general price index. Each year for the past several years, the members of the Association of Research Libraries (ARL) have spent 10% more for library materials than they did the previous year, yet the rate of growth of their collections has been only 3% per annum.[2]

---

*Richard W. Boss, *The Library Manager's Guide to Automation* (White Plains, NY: Knowledge Industry Publications, Inc., 1979).

Only a small part of the difference between rising expenditures and the growth of collections is accounted for by withdrawals of library materials. Since 1971, average yearly price increases have been 17.5% for U.S. periodicals and 11.6% for hardcover books.[3]

Labor costs are increasing 6% to 8% each year, with no significant rise in productivity. Construction outlays have risen so sharply that new buildings can cost up to $140 per square foot to build and furnish.

Library users' expectations are changing as well, a factor apparent in all sectors of librarianship. For example, problem-oriented research across many disciplines is becoming commonplace. Many users lack the time and background to search several indexes and abstracts in different fields. Consequently, they are relying more and more on libraries as intermediaries to obtain and evaluate the literature. This phenomenon is not unique to academic and special libraries: citizens' groups are using general public libraries to do research on such complex issues as environmental protection and the energy crisis.

Furthermore, library managers no longer hold the power that they were once perceived to have in the allocation of resources, assignment of staff and determination of new services. In many cases, staff members are exerting pressure to participate in the library's management, while other libraries are experiencing unionization. Increasing federal regulations on safety, equal employment opportunities and copyright protection also limit the manager's authority. As a result of these constraints, the decision-making process is more complex and time-consuming.

THE PAPERLESS SOCIETY

Some visionaries have forecast that libraries of the future will overcome the crisis by becoming paperless information intermediaries. Terminals in homes and offices will make library buildings with large seating capacities obsolete; mass electronic storage of bibliographic and full-text data will eliminate miles of shelving. This change to packaging information in paperless formats has been linked to library automation—libraries can't participate in this future scenario unless they install computers to gather scholarly information, organize it, store it and deliver it to users. Failure to automate will mean obsolescence.

A vice president of IBM has said:

> In our present 20th-century world of print and paper, we tend to think of information in terms of documents. In the future our information machines will permit us to enjoy more immediate access to all kinds of information-gathering capabilities. Documents will become only occasional by-products of information access, not the primary embodiment of it.[4]

It is also argued that the library will become "disembodied" because it will not contain any printed materials at all. It may be nothing more than a room containing a terminal. In addition, the librarian could operate just as well from an office near the persons served—whether on a campus or in the community.

These arguments are highly simplistic. The "paperless society" scenario overlooks the fact that libraries are repositories of the recorded knowledge of many generations. Today's library contains papyri, scrolls, books, journals, newsletters, phonodiscs, video tapes and magnetic tapes—each created in a different era, but each recording the knowledge of its own or of an earlier era, or both. In libraries, new technologies don't displace older ones; they augment them. The challenge for libraries of the future, therefore, is not to support a new electronic literacy but to support the "multi-literacy" that will be required of people in years ahead. The person who is literate only in the written word in the 1990s will be at a disadvantage, but so will the person who is literate only in the use of computer technology.

The makeup of future libraries will cause them to be more complex than ever. Besides bookstacks and reading tables, there will be carrels with computer terminals. The library may also support remote computer terminals with data bases that have been locally developed. An online catalog of the library's resources may be the first data base developed, but it is likely that other files of information, both bibliographic and nonbibliographic, will be put on a local computer. Information of local interest—or for which there is too small a potential user base to justify a commercial firm's offering the service—is also a likely candidate for the local computer.

CONSTRAINTS ON USE OF TECHNOLOGY

The rate at which all these changes will occur is difficult to predict. The diffusion rate for new technologies is much slower than many forecasters concede. Ten to 20 years may pass before a new technology is finally in widespread use. For example, the radio was initially regarded as a means for communicating with ships at sea, where the extensive system of telegraph wires could not reach; it was not used for land-based communication until 14 years after its invention. Similarly, the phonodisc was first limited to recording last wills and testaments.

There are many constraints on the diffusion of a new technology: technical limitations, economics, priorities in marketing, copyright restrictions, government regulations and personal attitudes. The following brief discussion gives examples of how these constraints are affecting widespread adoption of information technologies.

Technical Limitations

Some forms of graphics, such as photographs, scientific formulae or maps, cannot be accommodated as easily and clearly as letters and numbers. Much of the material now stored in libraries contains extensive graphics.

Lack of standardization is another—and particularly serious—technological problem. It is not yet possible to connect or electronically link automated systems purchased from different vendors, yet no vendor offers a complete family of equipment that can be used to scan existing printed text, enter and edit new text, index and retrieve it, electronically transmit it and reformat it as needed. Incompatible systems continue to appear. For example, by 1985 there may be five incompatible video disc systems on the market, even though the two already available in North America as of spring 1983 are not selling as well as anticipated.

Economics

In 1982 three major U.S. manufacturers announced their withdrawal from the computer bubble-memory market because they could not effect the economies of mass production that had been expected in 1979 when bubble memories were the sensation of the National Computer Conference. For publishers, the cost of conversion to electronic publishing is very high. They will have to invest not only in new equipment but also in time, so as to rekey or scan and edit the existing text. One major publisher recently invested $750,000 to convert a single reference publication to machine-readable form.

Marketing Priorities

The Kurzweil Data Entry Machine, an omni-font optical scanning device, might be ideal for converting large quantities of published information into machine-readable form, but Kurzweil Computer Products, Inc. (a subsidiary of Xerox Corp.) has identified only five major markets for the sale of its product over the next decade. Publishing and libraries are not among them. For the past few years, Information Systems Consultants Inc. (ISCI), a Bethesda, MD, library automation consulting firm for which the author is a senior consultant, has regularly taken pages of reference books and catalogs to Kurzweil in Cambridge, MA. Unfortunately, each time it has not been possible to get rapid and accurate scanning because the equipment has been designed to accommodate the idiosyncracies of legal documents, telephone directories and other materials that represent more attractive commercial markets. The company is not prepared to commit the time and funds to modify the equipment so that it can meet different needs.

Copyright Restrictions

Copyright holders may not permit the materials to which they hold the copyrights to be reformatted for electronic distribution. For example, a major microform publisher has recently been trying to renegotiate its microform republishing contracts so that it can use video disc technology when it becomes economically feasible. At first the licensors were willing, but when they became aware of some of the dramatic claims made for the new medium, they refused to grant the rights. They did not want to lose their print market or give up a potentially profitable option, which they themselves could exploit later on.

Government Regulation

The telecommunications industry has historically been highly regulated. Until recently, it was virtually impossible to enter the market to compete against AT&T because a company could not offer lower rates if it used the technologies envisioned in the Federal Communications Act of 1934. All rates for services covered under the Act were regulated by various agencies at the state and federal levels. Only when it was discovered that digital data—the form of information used by computers—could be transmitted over FM broadcast channels without adversely affecting radio programming and without falling under the Act was price competition introduced. AT&T's subsequent efforts to have the Act rewritten to cover new technologies resulted in a large number of computer companies seeking their own revisions that would facilitate their entry into data communication. The result was a standoff. When AT&T concluded that data communication would be an important part of its future, it began to respond positively to efforts to deregulate the industry in ways that would free it to manufacture and sell data communications hardware.

Personal Attitudes

Many publishers don't want to stop printing books and journals, and many library users resist the use of nonprint formats such as microform, video tape and video disc. At a meeting on information technology in 1977, sponsored by the National Science Foundation, several major publishers eloquently and emotionally expressed their fondness for the print medium. One economist attending the meeting observed that "a new generation of publishers will be necessary to adopt the future." Librarians currently seeking to save space by using microform frequently encounter pressures from patrons—especially older and influential faculty members in academic libraries—who want to obtain the printed materials.

THE GROWTH OF LIBRARY AUTOMATION

Despite the problems noted above—and many more examples could be given—technology will undoubtedly play a large role in the library of the future.

Electronic Library Systems

Already the technical services operations of libraries are being transformed. As of mid-1983 nearly 3000 North American libraries did electronic cataloging using the facilities of Online Computer Library Center Inc. (OCLC), Research Libraries Information Network (RLIN), Washington Library Network (WLN) and University of Toronto Library Automation Systems (UTLAS). Instead of locally cataloging each title at a labor cost of $10 to $40 per title, libraries draw on a shared data base of millions of cataloging records. Most libraries have to undertake expensive original cataloging only 10% to 15% of the time.

Automated acquisitions systems will soon be equally common. By mid-1983 more than 22 electronic acquisitions systems were in development or actually being tested by bibliographic utilities, turnkey vendors and major book wholesalers.

Automated circulation systems have been installed by more than 700 libraries, most of them turnkey systems from vendors who offer hardware, software, installation, training and ongoing maintenance for a fixed price. The first of these systems was installed in 1973—a time when the minicomputers on which most of these systems are based were still very limited in capacity. Since 1980 the circulation system vendors have offered integrated systems—on much more powerful minicomputers. An integrated system is a multi-functional system in which the functions share a common bibliographic data base. Virtually all requests for proposals (RFPs) issued by libraries in 1983 specified integrated rather than single-purpose systems.

Patron services, too, are being affected profoundly by technology. Increasingly, online data base searching is supplementing traditional reference services, particularly in academic and special libraries. Expanded interlibrary loan—one answer to the problem of tight acquisitions budgets—is facilitated by automated systems. The online public access catalog, still largely experimental, will appear in more and more libraries, enabling patrons to find the information they want more efficiently than they could through the old card catalog.

Technology will allow libraries to serve patrons in their homes, offices or schools. The Pikes Peak Regional Library in Colorado already allows patrons to use their home computers to search the library's online catalog. The University of Guelph, outside Toronto, has installed the hardware to enable dialing into the library system by any person with access to one of the campus' 150 computer terminals. In the future, the use of these libraries may go up, but the number of persons entering the library buildings may go down.

Electronic Information

Once libraries and their patrons are electronically linked, libraries may expand their electronic reference service. Professional skills are needed to search hundreds of available data bases, and even patrons with their own computer services are likely to need the help of trained searchers. In the future, the patron and the librarian may search computer-stored data bases together, even though they are not in the same room. This process is already occurring in one corporate library that cannot provide skilled searchers at every library location. The staff developed a "conference search," an electronic linking of two distant terminals searching the same data base. The librarian provides the searching expertise, and the patron the knowledge of the subject matter.

As full-text data bases with reference information become more common, patrons are discovering that they are collecting conflicting information from different sources. Therefore, they are turning to the librarian to perform a new role—that of validation and evaluation. On which data should the patron rely? The librarian can resolve the conflict in much the same way as conflicts among printed sources have been resolved in the past.

It is likely that some reference books will begin to appear in electronic form by the mid-1980s. Two encyclopedias have already been converted to machine-readable form and a number of directories are being redone. Such publications lend themselves to the electronic format because they must be frequently updated; it is often more economical to do this electronically.

Reference works in electronic format also make sense from a user's perspective. These are publications that are consulted only briefly and usually cannot be circulated from a library. Only a limited amount of the information is of interest to a particular user. For example, many users of the U.S. census data find that they can now do away with cumbersome volumes of tables. Instead, they can search a machine-readable file and retrieve data quickly. They can then manipulate the data to arrange them in the format in which they will be most usable.

Many of the titles found in the typical reference collection lend themselves to a format other than print. In a recent unpublished study, an academic library determined that of 13,000 volumes in its reference room, approximately 25% would be easier to use online, rather than as printed tools, and another 10% might be more attractive on an optical video disc. What percentage of publishers will decide to reformat in the next decade and produce their revised editions online or on video disc? Given the constraints noted above, probably a minority. Even the reference department, the library unit that will probably feel the greatest impact from electronic publishing, is apt to collect primarily printed information for the next one to two decades.

Considering all these factors, the library of the late 20th century will be very different from the library of today because it will contain a much wider variety of nonprinted materials—not because it will retire its print collections.

AUTOMATION: COSTS VS. BENEFITS

The cost-effectiveness of automation in libraries has not been clearly established. Libraries have very large bibliographic files, often consisting of hundreds of millions of characters. Only a small percentage of the file may be consulted on a given day. (Becker and Hayes[5] estimate as little as 0.1%.) This is in sharp contrast to the activity in many business organizations, where each item in a much smaller file may be consulted a hundred times as frequently.

There are, nevertheless, real advantages to automating. Automation usually speeds the rate at which work is performed and, therefore, reduces the unit cost of the work. It also relieves the staff of repetitive chores and improves the accuracy and integrity of files. Multiple entry of data can be eliminated, and data can be reformatted more quickly to accommodate changing needs.

It is extremely difficult to acquire just enough computer capability to speed up the work done manually without also acquiring capabilities that far exceed the needs of most users. Since many of these "extra" features are highly desirable, libraries tend to take advantage of them. The cost of performing a single task may be reduced, but total operating costs may rise because more work is done. Hugh Atkinson, while director of the Ohio State University Library, said:

> The reason for the inability of libraries to reduce budgets, of course, is that most libraries which are not "special libraries" have a vast reservoir of unmet needs. Whenever one reads of or otherwise examines new circulation systems...or any other expansion of library facilities or services, it is almost always mentioned that startling and dramatic increases in use appear. Whenever one examines the introduction of new methods of cataloging or acquisitions, increases in service can again be demonstrated.[6]

The cost of using computers is coming down rapidly, however. Each operation performed by a computer in early 1983 costs less than 3% of what it cost seven years earlier. This decrease, combined with the rising trend in labor costs, will make some degree of automation cost-effective for almost all libraries in the very near future. In 1983, however, the consensus among those who have studied the costs and benefits of installing computer systems remained that improved services are a more compelling reason to automate than are possible reductions in costs.

THE DECISION-MAKING PROCESS

The decision to make a major capital investment in automation—and the organizational changes that go with it—can be highly political. Some people may feel their jobs are threatened; others may resist a reallocation of resources. There are many who like the traditional library of books and journals and will resist attempts to change it even in the face of crisis.

One of the most significant decisions of a library manager's career is the decision to automate one or more functions of a library. This book's purpose is to describe the present state of automation, its value to libraries, future trends in automation and the role of the library manager in the process.

The author does not assume that automation is always the solution to a library's problems. A library must carefully define its problems and identify and evaluate all available alternatives. It must take care not to mistake the symptoms for the problem. For example, a large public library sought funds to automate circulation control because lines were forming at checkout desks. A brief review by a systems analyst revealed that the reason for the lines was not the slowness of the mechanical charging machines, but the fact that circulation clerks handled registrations and registration renewals as well as charges. By transferring all registrations to a separate window, the lines were virtually eliminated. While the library did go ahead with its plans to automate, the basis on which it was able to justify the investment was an anticipated reduction in the backlog in overdue preparation and in the great deal of time required to process reserves or holds.

ABOUT THIS BOOK

Automation is not solely a technological issue. Throughout this book, emphasis is placed on the context in which the technical decisions must be made. All of the steps in the process of making and carrying out the decision are covered; no expertise in automation is assumed.

Chapters 2 through 5 discuss the fundamentals of automation with which the library manager should be familiar: hardware, with particular emphasis on the central processing unit; software, which tells the machine how to do its work; the principles and technology of and the options for data communications; and—a crucial area, often overlooked—how to build and maintain the data base.

Chapter 6 describes the options facing libraries: purchasing a turnkey system, undertaking in-house development, sharing the system with other libraries, etc. It also discusses the problems of linking different systems and offers profiles of the leading turnkey system vendors.

Chapter 7 discusses planning and implementing in detail and makes suggestions regarding the role of library managers in the process. Cooperative planning and shared ownership, which may reduce the costs of automation, are also described. Implementation is treated from the development of specifications through bidding, contract negotiation, site preparation, delivery and acceptance to conversion of records and promoting support for the system within and without the library. Chapter 8 surveys future trends in automation and develops a profile of the library of 1990.

Appendix A is a directory of organizations that provide library automation products and services. Appendix B is a glossary of terms most often encountered in library automation. The bibliography offers suggestions for further reading.

FOOTNOTES

1. Paul Evans Peters, "United States Political Science Documents: Its Design Philosophy" (promotional leaflet, Pittsburgh University Center for International Studies, 1979).

2. "Research Libraries Collections Hit Hard by Inflation," *The Chronicle of Higher Education*, January 22, 1979, p.1.

3. Ibid.

4. Lewis M. Branscomb, "Information: The Ultimate Frontier," *Science*, February 12, 1979, pp. 145-146.

5. Joseph Becker and Robert M. Hayes, *Handbook of Data Processing for Libraries* (New York, John Wiley & Sons, Inc., 1970), p. 109.

6. Hugh Atkinson, "Personnel Savings through Computerized Library Sytems," *Library Trends*, April 1975, p. 587.

2

Hardware Basics

Every library manager should understand a few basics about computer hardware—the equipment with which work is done in an automated environment. Such knowledge is more important today than in the 1970s because much of the profit made by vendors of library automation today comes from the sale of hardware. A vendor, therefore, may seek to create a situation that will require the library to come back again and again for add-on and replacement equipment. For example, a small central processing unit with its maximum primary memory installed is less expensive than a larger unit with only part of its capacity installed. A vendor can benefit from this fact in two ways: by bidding the smaller unit, it may appear to have a more attractively priced system, and there is a good prospect that it will be able to sell a replacement unit within a few years. In the case of disk drives, there is more money to be made by selling several small drives rather than large drives that add up to the same capacity. The proper choice of hardware is important because it may affect not only a library's ability to expand the system to accommodate growth in activity, but also the addition of other functions or the extension of the system to serve other libraries.

In this chapter we will discuss the components of a computer system, starting with a brief overview and then considering each component in more detail. Chapter 3 will discuss software, the programs that make the system function.

OVERVIEW OF A COMPUTER SYSTEM

A computer is a device capable of performing systematic sequences of operations on data at high speeds without a human operator intervening during the time the data are being run. There are three basic types of computer. A full-sized or mainframe computer is a digital device that has a central processing unit (CPU), multiple input/output (I/O) devices and a primary memory storage capacity of at least 1 million characters. A minicomputer is a compact digital device that has a CPU, at least one input/output (I/O) device and a primary memory of at least 64,000 characters. A microcomputer is a complete computer processor manufactured on a single integrated circuit chip with a memory of at least 4000 characters and normally but one input/output device. There is a fairly direct relationship between the size of the primary memory and the computer's functional capability. The distinctions among mainframe, mini- and microcomputers will be described more fully below.

All computers have at least the components shown in Figure 2.1.

Figure 2.1: Components of a Computer System

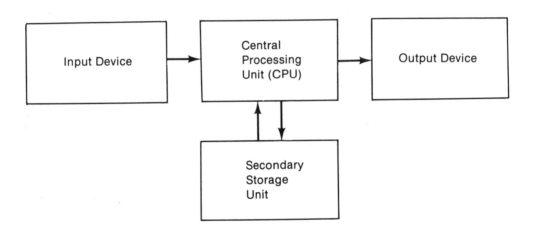

The Central Processing Unit

The central processing unit (CPU) is the heart of a computer system. The CPU can be conceptualized as having three components: control, arithmetic/logic and primary memory. The control section monitors and coordinates the activities of the system; the arithmetic/logic section does the calculations; and the primary memory or primary storage section contains the instructions programmed into the machine, the data to be processed, the result of preliminary calculations that are awaiting further processing and the data waiting to be output. In summary, the CPU controls all activities of the system, performs all calculations, stores and executes the instructions in the computer program, and holds the data while they are being processed.

The capacity of the CPU is usually quoted in thousands of bytes (K bytes or KB). Each byte is made up of a number of timed electric impulses called bits. The patterns of the bits create unique bytes or characters, some of them letters, some numbers. The smallest microcomputers hold 4K bytes (4000 characters) in the primary memory section, and the minicomputers most commonly used in libraries have from 128K to 512K bytes. In contrast, a large mainframe computer contains 1 to 8 million bytes (megabytes or MB) of primary memory. The greater the primary memory, the more programs can be held in the machine and the more data can be accommodated at one time.

Secondary Storage

The primary memory of the CPU is limited. It is, therefore, necessary to store much of the data used in processing in one or more secondary storage units, outside the CPU. The secondary unit consists of one or more disks or magnetic tapes mounted on disk or tape drives.

The CPU can automatically move data back and forth between the primary memory or storage section and the secondary unit. The separate storage unit offers a less expensive alternative to greater CPU capacity, but access is slower. The ability, however, to move data back and forth between the primary memory and secondary storage component makes it possible to handle larger programs and greater quantities of data on a small computer having a limited primary memory section.

The type of computer system determines not only the maximum primary memory, but also the maximum secondary storage. A mainframe computer can accommodate billions of characters of secondary storage. Minicomputer systems often are limited to 2.4 billion characters (2.4 gigabytes), and microcomputers may support as little as 1.25 million characters (1.25 megabytes).

Input and Output, Online and Offline

Data enter and leave the CPU through various input and output devices. A typewriter-like terminal is the most common input device. Other input devices include punched cards, paper tape and magnetic tape. Light pens and optical character recognition (OCR) wands have recently become major input devices. They are merely stroked over a label, and the bars or machine-readable symbols are read into the computer electronically.

The output device, which displays completed data, may be a typewriter printer, a cathode ray tube (CRT) for visual display, a magnetic tape unit, a line printer or a card punch. Both input and output devices are commonly called peripherals; they are linked to the CPU but are not part of it.

A peripheral device that is electronically linked to the CPU and that is using this linkage in a particular operation is said to be operating online. If a device is not connected to the CPU, or is not using the connection in a particular task, it is said to be offline. Thus, when a keyboard is being used to enter data into a storage device under the control of the CPU, it is operating online. If the same keyboard is used to enter data onto tape that will later be loaded into storage that is under the control of the CPU, it is operating offline.

BATCH AND REAL-TIME PROCESSING

The terms "batch processing" and "real-time processing" are commonly used to describe modes of data processing. A system operating in batch mode stockpiles data and passes them to the CPU for processing and output at a later time. In a real-time system, data are processed immediately upon entry, and all machine-readable files are simultaneously updated, often as part of the processing operation itself. Real-time systems thus maintain data files that reflect the current status of a particular application. Batch systems, on the other hand, do not provide such up-to-the-minute tracking because there is a lag ranging from minutes to days between the recording of a transaction and the processing of data relevant to the transaction.

All real-time systems are online systems, but a given online system may be operated in either batch or real-time mode. Online terminals may be used to enter data that become immediately available, or data may be loaded in batch mode using tape and then maintained on disks for online retrieval via terminals.

BITS AND BYTES

In computer terminology, a "character" is any letter, numeral, punctuation mark or other symbol encountered in data or software programs. A unique coding pattern is established to represent each of the characters to be recognized by the computer. While various coding schemes have been developed, most automated library systems are minicomputer-based and use the American Standard Code for Information Interchange (the ASCII code).*

ASCII employs the symbols "1" and "0" to express the pattern for each character. Such a code is known as a binary code because it uses different combinations of the two symbols to represent the various characters. Each appearance of a symbol in the code is called a binary digit or bit, and the combination of bits that encode a given character is termed a byte. Although the ASCII code uses seven bits to represent each character, an extra bit is usually added to each character string for error control, bringing the number of bits per byte to eight. Regardless of the number of bits involved, a byte represents a character in the computer system—whether a letter, number or another symbol.

As noted above, a computer's capacity—that of both primary memory and secondary storage devices—is measured in bytes and expressed as a number followed by the symbol K or KB. 1KB stands for 1024 bytes. A computer described as having 128K of main memory can store 128 times 1024 bytes or characters. In practice, the value of K is rounded to the nearest 1000, and the memory capacity is described in kilobytes or thousands of characters. It is, therefore, common to hear the expressions 128 kilobytes, 128K and 128KB. Very large CPUs and virtually all secondary storage devices have capacities measured in millions of bytes or megabytes (MB).

While the byte is the most commonly used expression of memory and storage capacity, computer capacity is sometimes described in "words," a measure that denotes the number

*Full-sized IBM computers use a different standard—the Extended Binary Coded Decimal Interchange Code (EBCDIC)—which is a more condensed code than ASCII.

of bits the control unit can retrieve from the primary memory at one time. An 8-bit-word computer can access 8 bits, or one byte (one character), at a time. The word lengths of available computing devices range from 8 to 64 bits, although most of the machines installed in libraries have 8- or 16-bit word-length capacities. When capacity is expressed in words, the same convention of using K for 1024 units (in this case words, rather than bytes) is followed. Word length is directly related to a computer's operating speed—the longer the word, the faster the machine.

To convert a statement of primary memory capacity that has been expressed in words to one expressed in bytes, multiply the number of words by the number of bits in each and divide by 8. Thus a computer with 64K 16-bit words of main memory can store 64 x 1024 x 16 bits, or 1,048,576 bits. Dividing 1,048,576 by 8, the equivalent character capacity is 131,072 bytes (nominally 128K bytes).

TYPES OF COMPUTERS

Depending on such characteristics as physical size, processing power, intended application and price, computers are typically categorized as full-sized, mini or micro. Full-sized computers are also often referred to as mainframes. The differences among the three categories have become increasingly difficult to discern, since minis have become as fast and powerful as many full-sized machines, and micros are beginning to rival the minis at the low end of the range.

From the late 1940s through the early 1970s, computer automation specialists emphasized the economics of size to be realized from using large-capacity computing equipment that would serve many users from a centralized facility. This argument was based on Grosch's Law, a principle articulated in the late 1940s by the computer scientist Herbert R.J. Grosch. The law states that larger—and consequently more expensive—computers provide significantly greater processing power per dollar than smaller, less expensive machines. Assuming that the additional processing power was required, Grosch's Law implies that the consolidation of computer capabilities in a single large CPU, rather than in several smaller ones, results in a lower unit cost of computer automation. By the mid-1960s, the development of time-sharing operating systems and telecommunications technology made such consolidation of computer resources feasible.

Grosch's Law was developed at a time when there were few inexpensive small computers. Most expenditures were multi-million dollar ones. Minicomputers were introduced in the 1950s but were used only in limited applications. Then, in the early 1970s, many computer users began to complain about the difficulties of dealing with seemingly unresponsive computer centers. They expressed a strong preference for more direct control over computer resources. Coincidentally, the replacement of transistors with integrated circuits, containing many miniaturized components on a single silicon chip, resulted in drastic reductions in the cost of minicomputers.

By the mid-1970s, many businesses and government agencies were using minicomputers to decentralize or distribute their computer resources and placing computers under the control of operating divisions or departments. A number of studies documented that Grosch's Law was no longer valid. Today the range of options is greater than ever, with CPUs costing from as little as $600 for a microcomputer to more than $8 million.

Mainframe Computers

Even mainframe or full-sized machines are now available in all sizes. At the top are the super-computers manufactured by companies such as Cray Research, Inc.—a firm little known outside the computer industry. They are very powerful, special-purpose machines designed for scientific or other research applications requiring extremely rapid execution of a high volume of complex calculations. A super-computer's word size is 64 bits; the operating speed is measured in fractions of a nanosecond (billionth of a second); and the primary memory capacity is measured in millions of characters. Prices for super-computers are usually in the millions of dollars.

Below the super-computers, most full-sized computers are properly characterized as large-scale or medium-scale machines designed to perform common scientific and data processing tasks. IBM Corp. is the dominant company in this segment of the market. Although large-scale computers are generally smaller than super-computers, they also access 64-bit words. They offer main memory capacity in the 4 to 32 million character range and feature operating speeds measured in nanoseconds. Large-scale computers have a great amount of parallel circuitry as well, so that multiple bits can be processed simultaneously. Thus, while a micro may process 8 or 16 bits at a time, a large-scale computer may process 32 or 64 at a time.

Prices for large-scale machines typically begin at around $500,000 and go to several million dollars. Medium-scale computers are somewhat smaller and slower, with the primary memory capacity beginning at 256,000 characters. Their prices start as low as $250,000. Several libraries, such as those at Northwestern and Ohio State Universities, have developed automated systems in-house, using large and medium-scale full-sized computers.

Relatively small full-sized computers are now available, priced from $100,000 to $250,000. Designed for common data processing applications, small full-sized machines have a primary memory capacity of 256,000 to 2 million characters. They access 32-bit words, and the operating speed is typically measured in microseconds (millionths of a second).

Minicomputers

Minicomputers can also be obtained in a wide range of sizes and speeds. The so-called "super-minis" are more powerful than some smaller full-sized computers: they access 32-bit words; operating speed is measured in microseconds or even nanoseconds; the primary memory capacity may exceed several million characters; and a mini can support the same types of peripheral devices as a full-sized central processor. (Companies such as Digital Equipment Corp. and Data General Corp. have called their largest machines super-minis when they could just as well have called them full-sized machines.)

The typical minicomputer features a 12- to 16-bit word size, an operating speed measured in microseconds and primary memory capacities of 128,000 to 1 million characters or more. It is able to support a variety of peripheral devices, including multiple online terminals. Virtually all of the computer systems that libraries have purchased from vendors who supply software as well as hardware have been minicomputers of this type.

Microcomputers

The mini is being increasingly challenged by the microcomputer or micro, a computer system that incorporates a microprocessor as its CPU. A microprocessor is a single-chip integrated circuit device capable of performing the operations typically associated with the control and arithmetic/logic sections of a CPU. Powerful, inexpensive microprocessors have been made possible by large-scale integration, a manufacturing technique whereby thousands of highly miniaturized circuits can be consolidated in a very small space.

Larger computers, computer terminals, calculators and appliances often contain microprocessors. These differ from those used in micros in that they are preprogrammed by their manufacturer to perform a specified task. Thus, they lack the programmable characteristic of the computer systems that libraries typically need.

Micros have become particularly popular for individual computer use. Until recently, the most popular designation for such a machine was "personal computer," but it is becoming more common to apply the term "professional computer" to a unit which can be used by only one person. The simplest personal or professional computers incorporate a microprocessor, random access memory circuits and a keyboard in a single unit designed to be attached to a television monitor. These systems are rarely suitable for use in a library.

Through the addition of memory circuits and peripheral equipment, small microcomputers can often be expanded into small business computer systems. Prices for the least expensive fully configured business-oriented microcomputer systems range from $5,000 to $10,000. These micros can access 8-bit words; operate at speeds measured in milliseconds (thousandths of a second); provide 16,000 to 128,000 characters of primary memory; and will support one terminal, one printer and a low-capacity disk or tape storage device. They are designed primarily for self-contained, desk-top operation. Priced at $10,000 to $20,000, more powerful microcomputer-based systems offer a main memory capacity of 64,000 to 256,000 characters. Several available micros can access 16-bit words; it is expected that these more powerful devices will eventually replace the 8-bit machines for business applications.

Multi-user, multi-tasking microcomputers hold the most promise for libraries because they can accommodate several terminals and the performance of several different functions concurrently. They are very much like minicomputers, except that they support fewer terminals and process data somewhat more slowly. The typical price is $25,000 or more, and the main memory is usually 128,000 to 256,000 characters. They often share the architecture, or physical design characteristics, of larger minicomputers, so that a user can migrate to the larger machine when necessary without rewriting of programs.

As of mid-1983, large-scale computers enjoyed a reasonable cost-performance ratio when many tasks had to be performed concurrently, and micros when a single task had to be performed continuously. The former situation is typified by a bibliographic utility, the latter by a small single-function serials checkin system. (The most successful applications for microcomputers in libraries have been for office and management uses such as word processing, statistical analysis, accounting or scheduling of staff.) Minicomputers generally were most cost/service-effective in the case of multi-function systems for individual libraries or small groups of libraries.

SYSTEM COMPONENTS

In the following pages, the function of the components in a computer system will be discussed in greater detail.

CENTRAL PROCESSING UNIT

The CPU, regardless of its size, contains three principal operating components:

• The *control* section directs the operation of the other sections, as well as the relationship between the CPU and its peripheral devices.

• The *arithmetic/logic* section contains the specialized electronic circuitry essential to computation. The CPU performs repetitive logical operations involving the testing of specified conditions or the comparison of data. In most information storage and retrieval applications, these logical operations are more important than the arithmetic operations for which computers were originally developed.

• The *primary memory or storage* section provides storage for data and programs within the CPU. CPU memory is often described as primary storage to distinguish it from auxiliary or secondary storage devices such as disks. The information stored in the primary memory is recorded in an encoded, machine-readable form that is essential for computer processing. Primary memory can be accessed more quickly than secondary storage because it is kept inside the CPU. Since it is substantially more expensive than secondary storage, primary memory is generally not used for long-term data storage.

Data are recorded in the central processing unit by setting the physical components of the memory device so that the CPU can "read" or detect the data. In the earliest computers, vacuum tubes were selectively switched on and off to represent the combinations of conditions that represent individual characters in a binary system. During the 1960s and early 1970s, the memory sections of CPUs consisted of small, circular metal cores that could be magnetized in either of two directions—individual characters were represented by the pattern of magnetization. This system is reflected in the term "core memory," which is often still used as a synonym for a computer's primary memory.

The memory sections of present-day computers generally store information electronically rather than magnetically: sections are composed of large numbers of highly miniaturized, random access memory circuits integrated on chips of silicon or other semiconductor material. Each circuit is capable of being in one of two states—conducting electricity or not conducting electricity. Thus, in a manner similar to that employed by magnetic cores, individual characters are represented by the presence or absence of electrical current in a specified combination of circuits.

INPUT PERIPHERALS

Input peripherals translate human-readable information into the machine-readable form required by the CPU. The information may be converted by a keyboard or optically scanned. The keyboard-oriented devices feature a typewriter-like keyboard on which the data are typed, character by character. The keypunch machine, which converts individually typed characters to a specified pattern of holes punched in successive columns of a specially designed card, has been substantially replaced by other forms of input devices. Other instruments offer greater operator productivity and avoid creating tubs of cards, which are often vulnerable to damage and spilling and require considerable storage space.

Keyboard Input

Key-to-storage equipment is currently used for entering data. There are two methods. The key-to-tape approach is based on a microprocessor-controlled device with a keyboard, a CRT screen and a magnetic tape recorder. Characters typed at the keyboard are displayed on the CRT screen and recorded on magnetic tape; errors detected during keystroking can be simply corrected by backspacing and overtyping with the correct character or characters. The typical key-to-tape machine produces a reel or cassette of magnetic tape, which must then be taken to a tape reader for input to a computer.

The key-to-tape method is being supplanted by key-to-disk equipment, now the most popular choice for data entry. This equipment consists of a CRT with a keyboard that operates online to a computer. Characters entered at the keyboard are transmitted directly to a magnetic disk where they are stored pending later processing. In many applications, the terminal displays a formatted screen with labeled areas designed to prompt and guide the operator in entering specific data. Some key-to-disk systems feature a sophisticated microprocessor-controlled "intelligent" terminal that can be programmed to perform certain simple data validation procedures prior to transmission.

Keyboard-oriented input is an error-prone activity—it is probable that 2% to 5% of the finished work will be incorrect, even if care has been taken to look for and correct errors on the screen during data entry. Common data-entry error-detection techniques include editing the information on the screen and double entry. This latter method entails retyping the material so that the computer can electronically compare, character for character, the second version with the previous version. Double entry is a highly effective method of detecting errors, since it is unlikely that the same keystroking errors will be made during both initial entry and rekeying (especially if a different operator types the second entry). But such verification virtually doubles the already high labor cost to enter the information.

Data-entry costs can often be significantly reduced by purchasing or obtaining existing machine-readable data, either by accessing them remotely or by loading them into the local system. Where the local conversion of information is required, however, optical recognition technology can often be used to minimize data entry labor by substituting electronic scanning for keystroking. This may also greatly reduce the error rate of entering data.

Electronic Scanning Input

Electronic scanning uses reflected light to determine the content of material. Once identified, the data are encoded and recorded on magnetic media or transmitted directly to a computer. Several types of electronic scanning devices are designed for special applications. One, bar code recognition, is well known in libraries and retail stores. Bar codes represent numbers by using the height, width and distance between marks to express characters. They cannot be read by humans, so the characters represented by the bar codes are usually printed next to the bars in numbers and letters. Several different bar codes are in use; the best known are Monarch's Codabar, the Universal Product Code (UPC) and Intermec's Code 39. Codabar is the one most widely used by libraries, because it has been offered by the major vendors, CL Systems, Inc. (CLSI), Gaylord Bros., Inc., Systems Control, Inc. and Cincinnati Electronics.

Bar code technology is suitable only for scanning a limited amount of information—typically no more than 18 characters. The bar code label may be affixed to documents, merchandise or other objects and is typically scanned by a pencil-shaped wand equipped with a photocell.

Used both for identification labels and for extended data entry, OCR is another type of electronic scanning technology. As the name implies, OCR uses reflected light to identify the individual character content of input documents—letters, numbers, punctuation marks or special symbols. Since these characters vary in size and shape, each will mirror light differently. An input device called an OCR reader scans the material and identifies individual characters by comparing their light reflectance properties with definitions already stored in the computer. The identified characters are then encoded in machine-readable form. Keystroking labor is eliminated.

In theory, catalog cards, patron registration cards and other typed documents could be scanned by OCR equipment. In practice, however, the range of acceptable input is quite narrow and varies considerably depending upon the particular OCR reader being used. Most of the available devices will only accept input documents prepared according to rigid format specifications and in type fonts specifically designed for optical recognition. Since most existing library documents were not prepared in a font designed to be read by machines, it may be several years before omnifont OCR equipment will make it possible to reformat material without keystroking. Most libraries now using OCR limit their application to scanning patron- and item-identification labels. Department stores and clothing stores often use OCR price tags, which can be scanned at the time of the sale.

OCR equipment does, however, offer certain advantages as an alternative to conventional keystroking in applications that require ongoing data entry, including library labels. Input prepared in OCR type fonts is both human-readable and machine-readable, and OCR data can be prepared on an IBM Selectric or equivalent office typewriter equipped with any of several available OCR typing elements. Therefore, OCR-oriented data entry is well suited to low-volume applications where an existing typewriter can be temporarily converted into an input station. When a library prints its own OCR labels, it can usually produce them for $.006 per label as against $.03 to $.04 per label when bar code recognition labels are purchased. There may be a higher rate of unaccepted scannings in the case of OCR labels, thus requiring a second scan before the data are entered, but no reliable data are available on this supposition.

Almost all libraries place their labels inside the front or back covers of permanent library materials. One West Coast public library has placed the labels on the outside of all books, on the upper left-hand corner of the front of the book, and has protected them with strips of clear tape. A number of libraries have put labels on the front covers of paperback collections. The labels last for at least a year, even on heavily circulated books; replacement is simple and inexpensive. Handling time is significantly reduced, both during first labeling and each time the item is circulated, because the book does not have to be opened.

OUTPUT PERIPHERALS

Output peripherals convert machine-readable computer-processed data into a form that we can read. Library automation relies on those output peripherals that print information on paper, record it on microform or display it on a screen. Even the computer systems that rely heavily on screen displays print on paper for backup or for producing extensive reports.

Printers

Available paper printers vary considerably in technology, output characteristics, operating speed and intended application. Historically, line printers have been the dominant output device in installations with full-sized computers. The typical line printer features a "printing chain," consisting of chains of characters represented on embossed metal slugs linked in an endless loop. Multiple hammers are activated simultaneously so that the device appears to print entire lines at one time. Other line printers employ drums rather than printing chains, but their output characteristics are similar to those of chain printers.

The most common print chains have 60 to 64 characters, including the upper-case Roman alphabet, numerals and the most widely used punctuation symbols. Special extended print chains have been developed for printing bibliographic data. Line printers accept continuous, fan-folded paper stock; each page measure 11 x 14 inches.

The rated speeds of available line printers range from several hundred to several thousand lines per minute, with full-sized computers generally supporting the faster models and minicomputer installations using slower devices with printing speeds of less than 600 lines per minute.

Variables like line lengths, page lengths and the size of the character set typically reduce a printer's rated speed. Thus, a machine capable of printing 1,000 lines per minute with an upper-case print chain will operate at half that speed if it must produce both upper- and lower-case characters. Operating speeds will be slowed even further by adding foreign characters or special symbols. Although line printers are many times faster than typewriters, they process data at a much slower rate than can computers. High-speed line printers range in price from $10,000 to $30,000.

There are also several categories of lower-priced, lower-speed line printers well suited to mini- and microcomputer installations. Most are priced in the range of $5000 to $12,000, and they include both impact and nonimpact printers. Some impact printers produce material of typewriter quality. Such units employ interchangeable wheel or thimble-shaped printing elements and operate at speeds of 20 to 50 characters per second. The print wheels usually provide upper- and lower-case alphabetic characters but lack the special symbols found on many of the more expensive line printers.

Another low-speed impact printer is the matrix printer. It prints individual characters from a matrix of closely spaced dots created by selectively driving a series of needles into an inked ribbon at speeds ranging from 30 to 180 characters per second. A group of related nonimpact printers employs selectively heated needles to print dot matrix characters on thermally sensitive paper. In either case, dot matrix output is legible enough to be used for charge-out slips, receipts or working copies of reports. The quality of dot matrix output is not generally considered acceptable, however, for the production of more permanent or formal materials such as bibliographies and final reports.

Computer Output Microfilm

Computer output microfilm (COM) is a variant form of nonimpact output technology in which information is recorded on microfilm rather than on paper. A typical COM unit is capable of recording document images at rates ranging from slightly less than 10,000 to more than 40,000 lines per minute. COM recorders usually cost more than $100,000, and because of this expense, most libraries use COM recorders operated by computer or micrographics service bureaus.

The image capacity of COM varies with the type of microform and the reduction employed. For example, if a 48-to-1 reduction is used, a single microfiche can contain as much information as 270 computer printout pages. At the same reduction, a 100-foot roll of 16mm microfilm can accommodate the equivalent of 7200 computer printout pages. Some COM equipment uses such formatting strategies as the elimination of frame borders to pack even more information onto the microform. Although earlier models were limited to the upper-case alphabet, numerals and frequently used punctuation marks, most newer COM recorders can accommodate both upper- and lower-case alphabets, accented characters and other symbols used in bibliographic data.

COM is often employed to create a backup medium or to store historical data from a computer system. In another typical application, the COM recorder is used to produce a master from which a duplicator makes multiple copies. These copies are then distributed and accessed, using COM readers.

Screen Display

Rather than printing human-readable information on paper or microfilm, a third class of output peripherals displays the results of computer processing on a screen. These screen-oriented output devices or video display units (VDUs) are most often configured or built with a keyboard to enable the VDUs to double as interactive computer terminals. Most video display units incorporate a television-like CRT mounted in a plastic or metal case measuring about 20 inches on each side. The CRT has a phosphorescent screen, typically measuring 9 to 15 inches diagonally, on which characters are displayed as light images on a dark background. Some devices allow reverse video, in which the user can display dark characters on a light background, a useful highlighting technique. With most newer devices, a filter in front of the screen reduces the glare that has contributed to complaints of operator eye fatigue. In most cases, dials or other controls permit a user to further adjust the contrast and intensity of the display to suit personal preference. Most CRT-based devices can display both upper- and lower-case alphabet characters, and some units can display foreign alphabets, accented characters or other special symbols encountered in bibliographic data.

CRTs are limited by the speed of the telecommunications link that connects the unit to the computer on which the data are processed. Most applications involve speeds in the range of 30 to 240 characters per second, although some CRT devices can display data at speeds of up to 1920 characters per second. CRTs are usually priced between $800 and $3000.

SECONDARY OR AUXILIARY STORAGE DEVICES

Secondary or auxiliary storage devices are designed to retain information in machine-readable form while awaiting computer processing. They supplement the necessarily limited capacity of the CPU's primary or main memory, which is reserved for the storage of programs and the data that the computer is processing at a given moment. In the absence of secondary storage, information would have to be reentered prior to each incident of computer processing, and applications involving large amounts of data could not be computerized at all.

Although early computer systems used paper media—such as punched cards or punched tape—for recording and storing machine-readable data, magnetic storage devices have now become the most widely used means of secondary storage.

Magnetic Tape

Magnetic tape is the most economical of the several types of auxiliary storage media. Employed in full-sized and minicomputer systems, the typical magnetic tape is ½-inch wide and 2400 feet long; it is wound on a plastic reel. Microcomputer systems also often include magnetic tape, in shorter lengths, inside a plastic cassette similar to the cassette used in audio tape recorders.

Regardless of its housing, the tape is divided across its width in parallel tracks, most commonly nine, with each track intended to record 1 bit. The accumulation of 8 parallel bits represents a single character. The ninth bit, called a parity bit, is used for error detection. Successive characters are recorded down the length of the tape in groups called blocks. The most common recording densities are 800 and 1600 bits per inch (bpi), although some devices record and read up to 6250 bits per inch. The characters themselves are typically represented in either the ASCII or EBCDIC code. The typical storage capacity of a 2400-foot reel of ½-inch magnetic tape is 45MB of storage. By comparison, a cassette tape usually stores no more than 200 to 500K of data.

Magnetic tape is actually the secondary storage *medium*. The peripheral *device* is the tape drive, which includes a take-up reel and a motorized mechanism designed to move the tape past read/write heads. These heads use electricity to record bits by magnetizing the tracks in a predetermined pattern or by sensing a previously magnetized pattern of bits. The most expensive tape drives will accept various types of tapes; others are limited to tapes recorded in a particular coding pattern or at particular densities. Although tape drives operate online, the tapes themselves are typically stored offline, hanging from racks, when not in use.

Because the recording or reading of data onto or from a particular portion of a tape requires that preceding portions also be moved past the read/write heads, magnetic tape is typically reserved for applications where data will be processed serially, in the same order in which they are recorded. Even though tape drives operate at speeds ranging from about 30,000 to several million characters per second, it may take several minutes to access a particular record. Magnetic tape is, therefore, not a suitable storage medium for interactive computer applications in which data must be accessed rapidly and at random rather than in their recorded sequence. Such applications must use more expensive direct access storage media. Of these, magnetic disks are the most common.

Magnetic Disks

A magnetic disk is a rigid, magnetic-coated platter on which data are stored, character by character, in a series of concentric tracks. In most cases, two or more disks, or platters, are aligned on a common spindle in a configuration called a disk pack. The capacity of disk packs varies with the number of platters and the density of recording and, at the present time, ranges from 10 million to over 300 million characters.

The magnetic disk is today the principal secondary storage device used in library applications. It is a high-density storage device, with its capacity measured in millions of bytes, or MB. Many smaller libraries use two 60MB disks, and some larger libraries have as many as four 300 MB devices. Because of the large data bases that libraries normally seek to maintain, the total cost of the secondary storage represents a larger percentage of the total system cost than does the CPU: a pair of 60MB drives is more expensive than the CPU to which they are attached.

In addition to the high cost, the magnetic disk is also relatively slow. Large CPUs operate inefficiently with magnetic disks because they have to wait for information to be retrieved from the disks. A disk pack consists of several layers, or platters, each with several hundred tracks of information. Each track is subdivided into sectors. A sector is the amount of data transferred when an access arm with a read/write head moves over the surface of the platter. Locating the track, finding the sector and transferring the data to the CPU takes time even when the disk controller is not currently occupied; but when data are already being sought, the queries stack up. In human time, only fractions of seconds are involved, but they can add up to several seconds of response time in the course of a complete search. Failure to consider this may lead to implementations with unsatisfactory overall performance.

Winchester Disks

A recently introduced disk development, the Winchester disk, uses thin-film technology that permits bit densities of 12,000 per inch, a significant increase over other disk packs. The Winchester disk features a sealed head-to-disk assembly that need not be removed. The read/write head moves only 50 microinches from the surface, balanced by a column of air to facilitate rapid scanning. In order to maintain access speed, large Winchester disk drives should have multiple access channels.

The sealed conditions of the Winchester disk provide important protection against contamination—the greater the bit density, the more data would be lost if the disk were damaged. As a result, Winchester disks are twice as reliable for secondary storage as regular magnetic disks.

Large-capacity Devices

Where a very large data storage capacity (multimillion or multibillion character) is required, new storage systems have been developed that employ magnetic-coated tubes or strips stored in specially designed data cells. These data cells provide a kind of online tertiary storage for information that is used infrequently and would otherwise have to be taken offline and placed on magnetic tapes. It is expected that optical digital discs will perform a similar function in future computer systems. Such discs, which now exist in prototype and resemble the video discs marketed for home entertainment use, store data in combinations of encoded bits that are recorded and read by lasers. Unlike magnetic disks, however, optical digital discs are not erasable.

Small-capacity Devices

As the small computer systems market continues to grow, the demand for low-capacity storage also increases. The most common storage medium is the flexible disk or "floppy." The floppy is either a 5¼-inch or an 8-inch platter that can be recorded on either one side or both sides. The read/write heads actually contact the surface of the disk, so wear can be a problem. Since surface wear creates debris on the disk, reliability is also reduced. A floppy typically contains only 1MB of information; but since these disks are not permanently kept in the disk drive, larger files that do not have to be maintained online can be stored over several disks for future use.

SUMMARY

A basic knowledge of how computer hardware works helps the library manager understand not only what a computer can do but also what type of system will be best suited to a particular purpose. The basic functioning of the CPU is the same, whether the computer is a mainframe, a mini or a micro, but the differences in capacity, processing speed and prices are significant. The majority of present-day library systems are minicomputer-based, but a few university and special libraries use mainframe computers—some stand-alone and many shared with other parts of the parent organization. Increasingly, microcomputers are being used in small libraries or for single applications. Input/output devices and methods for secondary storage of data also present a range of options in capacity, function and cost.

The fundamentals of computer software—the programs that tell the computer what to do and how to do it—will be discussed in Chapter 3.

3

Software

Software gives the computer both its "personality" and its power. The term describes the group of programs or sets of instructions that a computer executes to accomplish an assigned task. More concisely, the data contained in the programs, which are entered into the primary memory, direct a computer through a series of activities. While in use, software is stored in the central processing unit's primary memory; when not in use, it may remain in secondary storage. (Software is not usable while it is in secondary storage.)

Proper choice of software is crucial. It determines how well a library meets not only its current needs but also its future needs, especially if the library has to change hardware or if the original software vendor discontinues its support. This is because some software can only be used on a single machine while other programs may be transferred from one computer to another.

SOFTWARE AND FIRMWARE

It is possible to program a computer by setting the switches on the front panel. First the program must be written down in the machine's own language and then laboriously entered into the machine by manipulating the switches to create a series of electronic impulses. This was how all programs were entered into the earliest computers. Today it is common to prepare a program on paper in a shorthand form that is human-readable. The instructions are subsequently converted to machine-readable form through character-by-character keyboarding at a card punch or key-to-storage device. The resulting machine-readable program is then maintained on magnetic media from which it is loaded into the primary memory for execution.

Programs that are frequently used in a variety of applications—for example, an extended character set for library applications—may be permanently recorded in electronic circuits called read-only memories (ROMs) that are located in the CPU's primary memory section. Such programs, which are typically prewritten by the computer manufacturer, are called firmware to distinguish them from software that can be modified or transported from one machine to another. Most software is not permanently recorded in the computer because it would hinder the machine's versatility.

SYSTEM AND APPLICATIONS SOFTWARE

Software is usually categorized as system software or applications software. The former consists of programs that enable a computer to function and to control its own operations; the latter are programs that perform some user-specified task, such as charging out books or producing overdue notices. Most hardware manufacturers provide prewritten system software for their equipment. Although most applications software is now written and sold by firms that specialize in software development, many applications programs have been written by users themselves.

TYPES OF SYSTEM SOFTWARE

There are three basic types of system software: operating systems, utility programs and data base management systems (DBMS).

Operating Systems

The most important category of system software is the operating system, the set of interrelated programs designed to facilitate the use of the computer in developing and executing applications programs. In early computer systems, a human operator monitored operations and determined the priorities of input, processing and output. By the mid-1960s, computers were being slowed by the need for human intervention. Operating systems were therefore developed to let the computer manage its own operations.

An operating system accepts and responds to the commands submitted, sets up and schedules jobs, and handles related tasks that would otherwise have to be undertaken by the system's human operator. The operating system also:

• Identifies users and determines whether, and to what extent, they are to be given access to computer resources;

• Responds to user-entered commands that initiate the execution of specified programs;

• Allocates required hardware and software resources to the programs and controls their progress and termination;

• Acts on exceptional conditions (errors) that occur during the execution of a program and alerts the user with appropriate messages.

Most operating systems are developed by computer equipment manufacturers specifically for use with their equipment. In some cases, the manufacturer may offer several different operating systems to use with a given hardware configuration. Alternatively, operating systems for specific computers have been developed by companies other than the hardware manufacturer for direct sale to users. This is particularly true of micros. In the initial development of micros, it was common for manufacturers to provide proprietary operating systems. However, many microcomputer users have chosen to employ the CP/M operating system developed by Digital Research, Inc. or a third-party CP/M conversion kit as opposed to the operating system provided by the equipment manufacturer. This is because there is more software available for CP/M-based systems than for any other operating system. However, not all micros are CP/M compatible.

Available operating systems vary considerably in power and complexity. Although the simplest—primarily those designed for personal computers—handle one task at a time, most operating systems for larger computers are designed to support multiple users simultaneously. The more powerful operating systems are also capable of maintaining two or more programs in primary memory at the same time (multiprogramming) and executing two or more tasks at the same time (multitasking). Such systems are also capable of supporting multiple terminals. In addition, some operating systems are capable of multiprocessing, whereby the resources of two or more CPUs are applied to a given program. This can be important if a library outgrows its original system. Rather than purchase an entirely new, larger system, the library may find it more cost-effective to add a second, smaller computer for multiprocessing. CL Systems, Inc. (CLSI) has configured such systems using the Digital Equipment Corp. PDP 11/44 (a mini) and 11/23 (a micro).

Real-time operating systems are those that can deal with interruptions and requests from users at terminals at the moment they occur. They also are able to put lower priority work in the background and pull it into the processor when there is time available.

In summary, an operating system increases the amount of work that can go through the machine. Systems analysts describe this as "throughput"; people at terminals would normally call it "response time." An operating system requires from .5 to 5KB of primary memory.

Utility Programs

Utility programs perform tasks that are routinely required by computer users. As with other types of system software, they are usually supplied by computer equipment manufacturers or by companies specializing in software development. Among the most important types are those that copy data from one medium to another, such as from disk to tape. Some utility programs are designed to sort data into a predefined sequence or to merge two or more sets of presorted data, and several kinds facilitate the software development process by simplifying the work of programmers. Other utility programs assist in detecting and correcting errors or "bugs" encountered during applications program development. The amount of primary memory required for a utility program varies dramatically, depending on the support offered.

Data Base Management Systems

In the past decade, a new type of system software—the data base management system (DBMS)— has become a popular way of handling large files of nonnumeric data, including bibliographic information. This book uses the formal definition of data base management systems: "A data base management system allows multiple independent users to have concurrent access to a central repository of information."[1]

A DBMS eliminates data redundancy. Each bibliographic record has to be entered only once, as a DBMS permits access to the entire record through any of its fields, even if the need for a particular access point was not foreseen when the data base was created. Before the development of DBMSs, one had to either create separate files for each required access approach—author, title, subject, call number, etc.—or create multiple indexes to the bibliographic file at the time the data base was being developed. A DBMS provides the ability to modify—and even restructure—the data base without affecting existing programs or creating new file structures. This facility is known as data independence. This and other DBMS functions strengthen the data's integrity by protecting data against hardware and software malfunctions and unauthorized access or modification.

Shared vs. Private Data

The design and architecture of virtually all DBMS software packages permit multiple independent users to access common data. The term independent refers to people from different areas of an organization having access to the same information or data. When accessed by independent users, data are said to be "shared." However, if information is specific to (only used by) a single person or group, or to a very small number of users, the data are called "private."

When data are private, security features are built into a DBMS that control who has access to the data. Shared data and private data place different requirements on the functions provided by DBMS software; therefore, an organization must determine the needs of its users and how data flows throughout the organization. Suppose, for example, that budget information for each branch of a library system is private. This would mean that a librarian at one branch could not consult data about another branch.

Shared data are desirable when all users are entitled to the information. For example, holdings information would normally be shared throughout a library system. The use of shared data, however, raises important questions that must be resolved, such as who has access rights and update privileges.

The need to share data may also change over time. When a needs assessment is being conducted, the investigator(s) may perceive the data as private, but once the data become machine-readable and are available through online terminals, other organizational units may find use for them. Again, some concept of the organization's data flow and wide consultation with prospective system users will help clarify whether data should be shared or private.

Concurrent Access

Concurrent access means that multiple independent users may contribute to, maintain and/or retrieve information from the same data base. Concurrent access can apply to shared or private data. For example, data may be shared between acquisitions and cataloging departments but not concurrent: acquisitions may order an item one month and cataloging may process it the next. Although the bibliographic data are shared in this case, access is serial. If the user requires current data and the system supports an interleaving of transactions from both acquisitions and cataloging, the access to common data is concurrent.

In the early days of computer automation, sharing data on tape or in manual records was serial: only one user could have access at any one time. The need to provide users with concurrent access to the same data surfaced during the early implementations of online, terminal-based systems. The technical feasibility of concurrent processing came about at the same time. However, many vendors' operating systems did not provide the necessary support for concurrency until recently. Most DBMSs, therefore, were developed to provide control for concurrent access when used with operating systems that did not contain the needed features.

A DBMS is more important when several users are working with the data base at the same time than when data are accessed serially because concurrent users can more easily interfere with each other's use of the data base. A DBMS does require the use of considerable computer resources, but this can be justified by the benefits it provides. A DBMS is most useful in an online environment with large data bases and a need for concurrency.

Concurrent access requires that DBMS software protect data with security controls not commonly found in standard-access methods. If concurrent access data base protection and the ability to modify data base structure and data base records independently of one another are necessary, then a DBMS should be considered. If not, it may not be necessary to use a DBMS.

Integrated Data

Centralizing data is another common reason for adopting a DBMS. The concept of building a central repository of data is key to the concept of a data base. The design process for accomplishing this requires determining all the data fields needed for the various applications and eliminating duplicate information. The result is an integrated data base, which can form the basis for an integrated system, one that makes it possible to perform two or more applications using the same data base.

When an application does not include integrated data, using a DBMS is a high price to pay—in dollars and in computer resources—for the benefits received. Many of the design points of commercially available library software are based on the assumption that data integration is in fact a user's primary objective. Many noncommercial software packages available from other libraries do not assume the need for data integration since they were usually developed for a single application rather than as integrated systems.

Data Representation

If a data base is to represent useful information about the real world, it must reflect data as they exist in the real world. Programmers have for years forced data to appear as needed for the convenience of the computers, not the users. Data do not exist in the real world as fixed-length field entities, and yet in the data processing world they often do. In order for a DBMS to provide information to users with dissimilar needs, it must reflect data and their structure as the users require them.

Data about the same title may repeat from one to several times, depending on how many editions and copies a library has. If there are several physical pieces, the identifying information should be consistent. Conventional computer file processing techniques offer two common solutions: they create variable-length records, and they separate the data into master and transaction files.

Variable-length records were originally designed to handle the variable characteristics of data. The record is designed with a fixed-length portion describing fixed data and a variable portion, such as for additional copies or joint authors, that repeats based on an indicator that tells the programmer how many variable portions to expect. A problem with variable-length records is that the system must be told how long the maximum record can be. To do this, a decision has to be made on what the maximum number of variable portions of any given record type will be. This may be real or an educated guess. When the figure chosen proves to be less than the real-world maximum, another choice has to be made: reprogram the application, or prevent the recording of more than the arbitrarily set limit. Often the choice is, by default, the latter because of the sheer cost of reprogramming. The maximum record length now becomes a data processing restriction imposed on the data.

The second approach, separate master records and transaction records, is more commonly used to accommodate the variability of data. Since a separate record is used to record each occurrence, this technique does not suffer from the problem of fixed lengths described above. Fixed data are recorded in a master file. For example, in a circulation system, one record exists for each patron. The transactions appear on a transaction file. To tie these records together, keys on the various records are repeated. In this case, the key of the patron master record is repeated in each transaction record. This solution, however, causes a replication of data in many files.

A major drawback of repeated data is inconsistency. Redundant data require redundant input procedures and redundant maintenance and are often reported redundantly in displays or printout. This leads to the data being out of synchronization with other places they are recorded.

Redundant and inconsistent data can hardly be used to generate information. Because a DBMS presupposes the use of variable-length records and handles records by creating pointers between elements rather than repeating data, it reduces redundant data and aids the designers of the system in providing consistent data to users. If the data being studied do not repeat and are not redundant, inconsistent or viewed as structurally different for different users, then one should seriously consider using a DBMS. But it provides justifiable benefits only if data are actually needed, and conventional file processing methods have not met this need in the past.

There are a number of popular DBMS packages for full-sized computers. Among them, ADABAS, DOS/VS, INQUIRE and TOTAL are frequently offered as part of a turnkey system. Minicomputer conversions of many of these DBMSs are available as well. One of the most frequently used DBMSs for minis is MIIS/MUMPS, which combines an operating system, a DBMS and a programming language in a single package. (MIIS/MUMPS is discussed in more detail later in this chapter.) The dominant product in the micro field is MDBS, from Micro Data Base Systems, Inc. Any of the data base management systems must be used with a compatible operating system and programming language.

APPLICATIONS SOFTWARE: PROGRAMMING LANGUAGES

As noted previously, programs that instruct a computer in the performance of specific tasks unique to an organization are called applications software. They may be written in any one of several programming languages.

System software, too, is written in a programming language, but the term is most commonly used in connection with applications software. Because of this, and because the languages are best understood in relation to one another, all types of programming languages will be described in this section. Three other examples of system software—assemblers, compilers and interpreters—are included in this discussion, because they function as "translators" of programming languages and should be viewed in conjunction with them.

Computers can only process instructions that are encoded in machine-readable binary form. Programming manuals tell the programmer which binary codes to use to represent particular operations. (If the code has been written directly in binary form, the program is said to be written in machine-level language, a programming language that can be executed immediately by the computer.) The individual instructions comprising the program are typically punched on cards or keyboarded at an input terminal for storage on disk or tape pending loading and execution under the control of the computer's operating system. The entry, debugging and modification of programs is facilitated by utility programs and other system software.

Machine Language

In contrast to the tremendous advances in machine speed, miniaturization and versatility, the basic level at which most machine languages operate has changed relatively little over the past two decades. Instructions can be executed only if they are submitted to the processor's control unit as sequences of numerical codes. Moreover, with a small number of specific exceptions, the typical machine language instruction represents an activity that is trivial by human standards, offering no direct correspondence with our idea of a "step" in an overall problem solution. Even when support software is used, the writing of programs in machine-level language is a time-consuming, error-prone task. Today machine language is normally used only for writing system software where the cost is offset by the substantially greater machine efficiency of having a program that can be executed directly.

There is now a way to bridge the gap between what the programmer wants to say and what the computer is designed to recognize. That solution is the development of two levels of languages besides machine language: assembly language and higher-level language. These have been developed to save programming time.

Assembly Language

Assembly language is similar to machine language, but it has been designed to facilitate human understanding. Symbols and abbreviations, rather than 0s and 1s, are used to write programs. The software development process has been made more efficient by writing programs using mnemonic commands instead of binary codes. In assembly language, it is common to use mnemonic codes in programming, such as ADD, MOV (move) and STO (store). These commands are much easier for a programmer to remember than the machine-level counterparts, and the resulting program is obviously easier to read and correct. Frequently used instruction sequences can be combined into a single mnemonic code so that they can be invoked with a single command.

While they are easier to write, the individual instructions comprising assembly language programs must eventually be translated into the binary-coded machine-level language that the computer requires. This translation is performed automatically by the computer using a special program called an assembler, also part of the system software. The assembler program, which is typically obtained from the manufacturer of the CPU, is usually written in machine-level language. All computers support an assembler program of some type, although the assemblers of different machines are typically incompatible.

Because assembly language is close to machine language (in fact, it is sometimes called a lower or intermediate language), it is most often used in those situations where the programmer requires very close control over the internal operation of the CPU, such as when writing operating systems, sort/merge programs and other system software. While it is suitable for writing applications programs because it uses computer resources efficiently, assembly language is relatively slow to use from the standpoint of the programmer. Since hardware costs are dropping and programming costs are rising, programmer productivity is becoming more important than efficient program execution. As a result, applications software is now usually written in one of the so-called higher-level programming languages such as COBOL, FORTRAN or MUMPS. Among vendors of turnkey automated library systems, only CLSI uses a considerable amount of assembly language, although some other vendors have written small parts of their programs in it.

Higher-level Languages

Higher-level languages are further removed from machine language than assembly.

Whereas one assembly language instruction is usually the equivalent of one machine language instruction, a single higher-level language instruction may trigger a dozen or more machine language instructions. Many higher-level languages allow the use of English-language commands. In short, higher-level language programs are easier, faster and less expensive to develop than those written in machine or assembly language. The resulting programs, however, must be translated into machine-level language prior to execution. This translation is performed by the computer itself, using a special program called a compiler, as distinguished from the assembler used when an assembly language program is translated into machine language.

Prior to its initial execution, a higher-level language program, called the source program, is translated by the compiler into the corresponding machine-level form, known as the object program. A variant form of the compiler called an interpreter avoids this step and translates individual instructions into their machine-level equivalents as they are encountered during the execution of a higher-level language program. As a rule, higher-level languages that use interpreters execute more slowly than those that use compilers, since instructions that initiate repetitive operations must be retranslated by the computer each time they are encountered. Their economic advantage is that they increase programmer productivity. Like assemblers, both compilers and interpreters are system software and, as such, are typically obtained from computer equipment manufacturers.

Machine and assembly languages are normally usable only on the single computer for which they were developed, and programs written in them can be run only on that particular machine. Higher-level languages are less machine-specific and offer much greater transportability from one machine to another with a minimum amount of rewriting. Machine language requires no storage of programs in primary memory; assembly language requires virtually none. In contrast, compilers for languages such as BASIC or interactive FORTRAN may use up to 12KB of primary storage. Thus, as a language becomes more user-oriented, it becomes less machine-oriented. One trades off human time against the cost of using additional machine capacity. Again, because programmers' wages have risen dramatically while the cost of CPUs has dropped sharply, this trade-off has become very attractive in the last few years.

The effective insulation between machine and programmer created by higher-level languages has had a profound impact on the increase of computer users and the range of successful applications. Most programs are now written in a higher-level language, and most people who write programs are no longer computer specialists.

EXAMPLES OF HIGHER-LEVEL LANGUAGES

There are hundreds of higher-level programming languages currently in use. Since their introduction in the late 1950s, these languages have tended to be identified with particular types of applications. Some are intended for use over a wide range of applications; others address themselves to a more limited spectrum of problem types characteristic of a specific discipline.

All higher-level languages, however, share a common property: the elemental vehicle for expressing the programmer's intention (i.e., the individual language statement) is constructed to convey a level of complexity consistent with the nature of the procedure being represented. In other words, the activity described in a single "instruction" or "command" bears no direct resemblance to a single machine operation. Instead, a higher-level language statement has substantial similarity to its counterpart in English or whatever notation is appropriate to the area of application.

The following are examples of widely used higher-level languages.

FORTRAN

The earliest higher-level languages were designed for technical applications. FORTRAN (an acronym for FORmula TRANslator) is the best known. FORTRAN instructions are written in an algebraic notation that is well suited to the mathematical problems encountered in the physical sciences, engineering, statistical analysis, the social sciences and business.

FORTRAN compilers are available for computers of all types, although programs written for execution on a given computer system will not necessarily execute well on other systems. Although FORTRAN standards have been developed by the American National Standards Institute (ANSI), most compilers deviate from the standard by offering additional features designed to enhance the language's utility. FORTRAN compilers developed for microcomputers usually cannot accommodate all of the instructions available with compilers designed for mainframe or minicomputer installations. FORTRAN was used by Cincinnati Electronics in its CLASSIC circulation control system until the company withdrew from the library market in early 1983. Gaylord Bros., Inc. uses a combination of FORTRAN and assembly language for its minicomputer-based systems.

COBOL

COBOL (COmmon Business Oriented Language) is the most widely used higher-level programming language for applications involving business data processing. Unlike scientific computing with its complex mathematical calculations, business applications are typically characterized by the repetitive performance of fairly simple computations involving large amounts of data. As a result, COBOL instructions emphasize data handling and report production. COBOL instructions are written in an English-like notation designed for simplified reading. As originally developed by a committee of computer manufacturers and users, COBOL was intended to be as machine-independent as possible. However, it is usually not used on small minis and micros because the large number of instructions in COBOL means that the computer, in turn, must have a large primary memory.

COBOL standards have been adopted by ANSI, but some versions offer enhancements not included in the standards. As a result, though COBOL compilers are available for virtually all mainframe and minicomputers, a COBOL program written for a particular computer system cannot always be executed on others. Again, as with FORTRAN, COBOL compilers developed for microcomputers typically respond to only a subset of the instructions included in the mainframe or minicomputer implementations.

DataPhase Systems has selected COBOL as the programming language for its large ALIS IIe library system, which is built around the powerful Tandem Computers, Inc. supermini. COBOL is also used by Sigma Data Computing Corp., the vendor that specializes in automated acquisitions systems for corporate and federal libraries. The Virginia Tech Library System (VTLS), which is now marketed as a software package for libraries not wishing to have the full range of services offered by a turnkey vendor, is also written in COBOL. International Computers Limited's (ICL) CADMUS—the turnkey system briefly offered by a major British computer manufacturer—also used COBOL.

String-processing Languages

While library automation applications share many of the characteristics of business data processing, bibliographic processing often requires the complex manipulation of character strings which may have no numeric values. The conventional higher-level languages such as FORTRAN and COBOL were designed to handle numeric information and brief records. Where more complex bibliographic records are to be manipulated, a group of string-processing programming languages such as SNOBOL4, COMIT or LISP can be used. Unfortunately, most programmers are not familiar with these, and few computers manufacturers support them. In addition, most string-processing languages use interpreters rather than compilers to translate the instructions into machine-language. As previously noted, programs written in interpretive languages tend to execute slowly and can prove costly because computer efficiency is poor.

MIIS/MUMPS

There is an exception to the general rule that the use of interpretive languages leads to inefficiencies in processing. Systems analysts working with medical records developed an approach that minimizes the sacrifice of processing speed. Now known as MIIS (Meditech Interpretive Information System from Medical Information Technology, Inc., or Meditech), it is an interactive, general-purpose operating system that contains an interpretive programming language (MUMPS, an ANSI standard language) and a complete set of data base management and programmer-aid utilities. It is, therefore, a combination operating and applications programming language geared to working with character strings, such as those common in bibliographic records.

In 1980, a survey of software users by Datapro Research Corp., a division of McGraw-Hill Book Co., concluded that the overall satisfaction rating of MIIS users was 3.82 on a scale of 4.00. An early user of MIIS was the Lister Hill Center for Biomedical Communications (National Library of Medicine), the developer of the Integrated Library System (ILS). ILS is available without support from the National Technical Information Service, and is also offered by two turnkey vendors. (See the section on bibliographic utilities in Chapter 8.) Another MIIS user is DataPhase Systems for its Data General-configured systems.

PL/1

Although the higher-level programming languages discussed to this point have been developed for specific types of applications, PL/1 was designed with generality in mind. This programming language combines FORTRAN-like mathematical capabilities with COBOL-like data handling facilities. Some string-processing facilities are also included. The resulting broad applicability has proven attractive to organizations that have to support a variety of operations.

Originally implemented on the IBM System 360 and 370 series of full-sized computers, PL/1 compilers have since been developed for the full-sized computers of other manufacturers. Some minicomputer systems offer subsets of PL/1 or proprietary languages patterned after PL/1. (Proprietary languages are unique to the developer and not generally available for use by others.) Only limited microcomputer implementations were available in mid-1983. DOBIS/Leuven, a library applications software package available from IBM, uses a combination of PL/1 and an assembler.

BASIC

All of the programming languages discussed up to this point were originally developed for preparing programs off-line—the programmer wrote the program, put it on the machine, ran it and then made corrections. With the development of online systems during the 1970s, programmers began working at terminals, and programming languages were introduced that returned results immediately. BASIC (Beginner's All-purpose Symbolic Instruction Code) is the best known and most widely used of these "online" languages. It is easy to learn and, although employing a FORTRAN-like algebraic notation, it can be used for both scientific computing and business data processing. Some versions also include very rudimentary string-processing capabilities.

BASIC has been used on a wide range of mini- and microcomputers. However, since it has not been standardized, there are many versions. Record-handling capabilities in BASIC are often more limited than in other higher-level languages; therefore, access to records is slower. In versions that use an interpreter, BASIC also tends toward slow execution. With some computer systems, however, BASIC is available in a faster compiler version. BASIC is used by CTI Library Systems, Inc.; BASIC Plus by Universal Library Systems; and BASIC Plus 2, a later version, by the Pikes Peak Regional Library District in its Maggie's Place software package.

PACKAGED APPLICATIONS SOFTWARE

The development of applications software has typically been the user's responsibility: that is, it generally doesn't come from the computer manufacturer, but must be developed in-house or purchased from another supplier. Most users no longer write their own software because the process is too time-consuming and expensive. Instead, they purchase packaged or prewritten software. A comprehensive software package developed by a commercial vendor may represent an investment by the developer of $500,000 to $1 million.

Only when this cost is absorbed by several customers are such comprehensive, sophisticated software packages affordable for libraries.

The major sources for packaged or prewritten applications software are hardware manufacturers, software houses that specialize in writing and selling applications software or turnkey vendors who supply software as part of a complete hardware and software package for a specific application. Libraries can also purchase software from other libraries that have developed their own programs.

Of the major hardware manufacturers, only IBM actively markets a library-software package: DOBIS/Leuven. No software houses offered a library applications package in mid-1983, but several library-produced software packages were available, among them Maggie's Place (Pikes Peak Regional Library District), NOTIS (Northwestern University Library) and VTLS (Virginia Tech University Library). Of the five largest turnkey vendors—CLSI, CTI Library Systems, Inc., DataPhase Systems, Geac Canada Ltd. and Universal Library Systems, Ltd.—only Universal actively markets software separate from hardware.

SOFTWARE DOCUMENTATION

When prewritten software is obtained from any source other than a turnkey vendor, it is usually necessary for the purchaser to assume some responsibility for ongoing software maintenance and enhancement. To do this, the purchaser needs documentation, i.e., detailed written information that is recorded during the development of the software and that explains pertinent aspects of the system.

Software documentation should be an integral part of defining and programming a computer system. However, a commitment to good documentation is costly. As much as 20% to 40% of the total development effort may go into documenting a new system— detailing how it is to work and how it was developed.

During the development of a computer program, documentation of how the program was designed is essential so that all people involved in a project will know what has been done and also so that they can pass information from one person to another, should staff changes occur. In addition, documentation may be important to prospective purchasers of the software because it facilitates evaluation and provides a basis for making subsequent changes in the software.

Documentation is essential not only to software design but to its subsequent maintenance as well. Effective continuing maintenance of the software demands that documentation be brought up to date when testing of the system is completed, to reflect any changes made as a result of the tests.

The systems analysts and programmers involved in a given software development effort are normally responsible for preparing appropriate documentation. Although most programmers recognize the value of documentation, under the pressure of a tight schedule, many programmers neglect to fully document software development activities. This particularly occurs when a software development effort is "over budget." Unfortunately, limiting the amount of documentation is often viewed as a way to achieve greater economy in program writing, and a software buyer may discover this only after beginning work on purchased software. Poor documentation then leads to significant increases in the time and costs associated with program maintenance and use.

If software is bought as part of a turnkey system, the vendor is required to care for the software. When applications software is purchased from a computer manufacturer, software house or another library, the buyer is usually responsible for continued maintenance and enhancement. Since maintenance programming accounts for more than half the software development workload in many organizations, there is a distinct advantage in selecting the type of software that is most easily maintained. Furthermore—given the changing requirements of users and the rising programmer turnover rate—"maintainability" has become a major factor in most software developers' decision to abandon assembly-language programming and use higher-level languages that employ readable English-like instructions, which are more readily understood by programmers.

At a minimum, the documentation for either custom-developed or packaged software should include the following components:

1. *System specifications* indicate the capabilities of the system and may be developed by the end user when a custom-developed system is being planned. More commonly they are prepared by the developer of a software package as the first step in the software design.

2. *Programming documentation* describes exactly how the system works. Without such documentation—usually prepared by the programmer actually writing the code—making changes to the programs may be difficult, prohibitively expensive or impossible. Programming documentation has four elements:

   a. *Record layouts* specify the arrangement of data within records. The layouts may be represented in graphic form, written in descriptive form or shown in some combination of these two. The length of each field should be given and whether it is numeric, alphabetic or both, whether it is used as a search key, etc.

   b. *Logic charts or descriptions* specify the processing flow and the decisions made in the programs. They may take the form of block diagrams or flowcharts, decision tables or narratives.

   c. *Program listings* are the actual source code listings that show the programming language instructions. They should be the latest listings and represent the actual object programs or machine-executable programs. All modifications should be included on these listings.

   d. *Program narrative* is the programmers' description of what the program does. At minimum, there should at least be an abstract of the program. Programmers vary in the extent to which they provide this documentation. Often, if the logic charts are complete and clear, there is little need for an extensive description.

3. *Documentation of testing* serves both as evidence of the tests that the system has already passed and as a good starting point for testing after any future modifications. This documentation proves that the system at one time performed properly. When later modifications are made, it is important to know that the system still performs the original functions accurately. Testing documentation should include the programmer's test data and final results and the user's test data and final results (including the original test, the error-routine test and the actual operational test).

4. *Operator's manual* contains complete instructions for loading and running each program within the system, as well as instructions on how to set up all equipment, how to process each type of transaction, the meaning of the error messages and the appropriate action to be taken when an error message is received. The manual should also specify appropriate backup procedures including the suggested frequency with which data should be copied for backup. The manual should incorporate sample input and output for each type of transaction.

5. *Procedures manual* is written by the end user, since it integrates the computer system into an organization's internal procedures. This documentation comprises such things as data entry instructions, schedules of when output is due, how frequently the user has chosen to perform the backup routine, etc.

Documentation is probably the least favorite activity of programmers, with the result that complete, up-to-date documentation will only exist if the end user insists on it. An RFP for procuring a turnkey system or a software package should therefore specify that detailed documentation be provided.

Software documentation is particularly important when purchasing a software package developed by another organization for its own use. Good quality commercially produced software is usually generalized and provides tables that permit users to tailor the system to their own requirements. Software developed by an organization for itself is often less flexible and will have to be modified by the buyer. Unfortunately, many software packages developed without future sale to others in mind are seriously deficient in documentation. It may, therefore, take the new owner a great deal of time to develop the documentation.

Even with inexpensive software packages for micros, adequate documentation is needed in order to make modifications, yet more often than with larger system packages, it is lacking.

SUMMARY

Software can generally be categorized as system software or applications software. System software controls the functions and operations of the computer and includes operating systems, utility programs and data base management systems. Applications programs are written to perform specific tasks desired by the user, such as circulation control.

In order for a computer to process any program, the software must be encoded in computer language. System software is usually programmed in machine-level or assembly language. Most applications programs are written in higher-level languages, which more nearly resemble English and so are easier to use.

Whenever maintenance or enhancement of software will be the responsibility of the library, the library manager should take care that adequate documentation can be obtained.

Chapter 4 discusses data communications, the electronic transmission of information between remote terminals and host computers or between computer systems.

FOOTNOTE

1. *Encyclopedia of Computer Science*, first ed. (New York: Van Nostrand Reinhold Co., 1976), pp. 391-392.

4

Data Communications

The term "data communications" encompasses the electronic transmission of information from one location to another and includes all physical equipment, software and procedures used in transmitting and receiving data. During the 1980s, increasing numbers of remote terminals will be linked to computers, and there will be a greater emphasis on the interconnection of computer systems to transmit information. Data communications for libraries will generally continue to be done using the existing telecommunications facilities, particularly telephone lines. Cable systems may also be in wider use for data transmission by the end of the decade.

MINICOMPUTER VS. MAINFRAME SYSTEMS

This chapter discusses data communications in general terms but emphasizes minicomputer communications because most automated library systems are minicomputer-based. Mainframe computers and minicomputers communicate differently; the former normally use synchronous transmission, the latter asynchronous. Synchronous transmission requires an internal clocking mechanism at each end of the communications channel to synchronize the transmitter and the receiver. Synchronous transmission uses communications media more efficiently than asynchronous transmission, but the terminals and communications equipment are usually more expensive. Costs are also higher because the remote terminals linked to a full-sized computer are often widely dispersed. For example, the majority of the terminals that are linked to a computer in a typical Fortune 500 company are more than 1000 miles from the central computer.

In contrast, mini-based systems are typically concerned with communications over relatively short distances of under 100 miles—often, in fact, of only a few hundred feet. Users generally require a limited number of linkages rather than a complex, multinode telecommunications network.

Moreover, the asynchronous terminals on most mini-based systems are "dumb" terminals, whereas the synchronous terminals of most mainframe systems have some built-in communications protocols. This distinction is particularly significant to telecommunications. Communications protocols, or standards, permit several terminals to be "multi-dropped" or grouped on a single telephone line because each terminal can be selectively "polled" or addressed by the computer. (One widely used standard is BISYNC, developed by IBM Corp. for its full-sized computers.) Minis are typically configured with one terminal per computer port so that the computer does not need to ascertain which terminal is transmitting.

A "dumb" terminal uses no communications protocol. It is a Teletype or Teletype-compatible terminal that displays or prints data just as it receives it. A dumb terminal may incorporate a microcomputer for data reformatting and other local activities, but it is still dumb if it is Teletype-compatible. Without a protocol, a terminal cannot be polled, so it cannot be clustered with other terminals on the same telephone line unless linked to additional equipment that contains a communications protocol. (An example of this is the multidrop concentrator, described later in this chapter.)

As noted above, most library systems are minicomputer-based, and many of the terminals are located within a few hundred feet of the computer site. These terminals thus can be "hard-wired," or directly connected to the computer. The usual connection is a simple twisted pair of wires using line drivers (signal converters that condition the signal to ensure reliable transmission) on each terminal and its associated computer port. Twisted pair wires may be installed by the telephone company, the computer system vendor or the system user.

When there is a need to link remote terminals, options are limited because there is no standard communications protocol for minicomputers. As of mid-1983, there were also no industry-wide protocols for microcomputers. The mainframe protocols exist because manufacturers had enough users with numerous terminals distant from their mainframe computers to warrant the development of protocols by the vendors.

Remotely located terminals are usually connected to the minicomputer by a telephone line with modems at each end. (AT&T uses the term "data set" rather than modem.) A modem (modulator-demodulator) or data set is an electronic device that converts the signal from the digital form used by computers to the analog form used for telephone voice transmission. The signal is modified to appear to the telephone system as a voice communication. Analog and digital signals are described in more detail later in this chapter.

Before discussing modems and other telecommunications hardware further, it is necessary to describe the technology of data transmission in greater detail. Fundamental to this is an understanding of the problems inherent in the transmission of data.

TRANSMITTING DATA

Any telecommunications medium distorts the data transmitted over it. A square-edged data pulse becomes a wavy line with all the voltage transitions slurred at the receiving end, as shown in Figure 4.1. As the transmission speed is increased, the distortion becomes greater; and as the distance of the transmission is increased, the impulses also fade.

Figure 4.1: Distortion of Transmitted Impulses

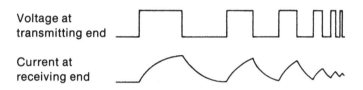

In addition, there is noise on the line from external vibrations. At high transmission speeds, the strength of the received pulses becomes comparable in magnitude with this vibration "noise," and errors in the interpretation of the data will occur. In all electronic circuitry, there is also a steady continuing background of internal random noise, sometimes called "thermal noise." As the atoms in the communications medium vibrate, they send out electromagnetic waves resulting in a chaotic jumble of electromagnetic waves of all frequencies that forms an unavoidable noise background to all electronic processes.

If the signal being transmitted fades too much, it becomes irretrievably mixed with the thermal noise. Once this occurs, the two can never again be separated. And if the signal is amplified, the noise will be amplified with it. Furthermore, if data are transmitted too quickly or too far, the signal drowns in the noise. (The longer the transmission distance, the more restricted the speed at which data can be sent.)

Given these factors, how should a channel for transmitting only computer, or digital, information be built? Typically, the user wants to transmit as much data as possible over an ordinary pair of wires, sometimes for long distances, and at a high speed. The solution is to install bit repeaters at intervals along the line. A repeater is a power-driven device that detects the bits being sent and then retransmits them with their original strength and sharpness. It catches the bit stream before it is submerged in noise and separates it from the noise by creating it afresh. Consequently, a very high bit rate can be transmitted, provided that the repeaters are sufficiently close together to catch the bits before they are lost in noise. On a communications line, the repeaters can be small, inexpensive solid-state devices.

ANALOG VS. DIGITAL TRANSMISSION

There are basically two different ways in which information of any type can be transmitted over telecommunications media: analog or digital. As noted, computer-generated information is digital. However, the most widely available telecommunications medium—the telephone system—uses analog signals.

In analog transmission, a continuous range of frequencies is generated. Light, sound, radio waves and the signals passing along telephone wires are all described in terms of frequencies. In all these means of transmission, the signal at a given point oscillates rapidly, just as a plucked musical instrument string oscillates. The rate of oscillation is referred to as the frequency and is described in terms of cycles per second.

Normally the sound—or light—reaching the senses does not consist of one single frequency but of many frequencies or of a continuous band of frequencies all traveling together. When we see red light, it is not one frequency but a collection of frequencies that combine to give a particular shade of red. Similarly, the human voice consists of a jumble of different frequencies. The same is true with the electrical and radio signals of telecommunications. Usually there is not one single frequency but a collection, or a band, of frequencies occupying a given range. A musical recording engineer strives to reproduce accurately a continuous range from 30 to 20,000 cycles per second. In turn, if high-fidelity music were to be faithfully transmitted over telephone wires into a home, it would have to be sent as a continuous range of frequencies from 30 to 20,000 cycles per second. The current transmitted over the wire would vary continuously in the same way as does the sound.

Digital transmission, on the other hand, means that a stream of bits—on/off pulses—are sent in the same manner that data travel in computer circuits: noncontinuously. It is possible today to transmit such data at an extremely high bit rate, except over voice-grade or analog telephone lines. However, digital phone lines exist in only a few areas. As noted above, modems are used to convert digital signals into analog signals for transmission over telephone lines.

A transmission path can be designed to carry either analog or digital data. This applies to all types of transmission paths—wire pairs, high-capacity coaxial cables, microwave radio links, satellites and new transmission media, such as fiber optics. If the path is designed to be analog, it will use amplifiers somewhat similar to those in a hi-fi unit for increasing the signal strength. (Unfortunately, these amplify noise and distortion as well as the sound waves and therefore function less effectively than bit repeaters.) If the path is digital, it will use bit repeaters to regenerate the bits and pass them on.

BANDWIDTH

The different physical media used for telecommunications vary widely in their transmission capacity. A multiwire coaxial cable, for example, can transmit far more information than a simple pair of wires. Analog links, such as most telephone lines, can handle differing data transmission rates depending on the characteristics of the modems used. A medium's capacity is referred to in terms of bandwidth.

Bandwidth, one of the most important terms in telecommunications, refers to the range of frequencies that a channel can transmit. If the lowest frequency a channel can transmit is f_1 and the highest is f_2, then the bandwidth of that channel is f_2-f_1. Bandwidth is quoted in cycles per second or "hertz." (Hertz means exactly the same as cycles per second. It is a more modern term that replaced cycles per second in the early 1960s.) Kilohertz (kHz) means thousand cycles per second, and megahertz (mHz) means million cycles per second.

The bandwidth of a telephone channel is about 3 kilohertz and normally transmits frequencies from about 300 to 3400 hertz, the range needed for transmitting the human voice. Often special techniques can raise the frequency base to high frequencies over 80,000 hertz, but this does not change the bandwidth, which remains 3 kilohertz. Bandwidth, then, says nothing about the frequency of transmission; it only indicates the range of frequencies.

The capacity of a channel for carrying information is proportional to its bandwidth. A channel with a bandwidth of 30 kilohertz can carry ten times as many bits of computer information per second as a telephone channel of 3 kilohertz. If the speed of transmission were doubled, the time needed to relay the data would be halved. Doubling the speed doubles the frequencies of the sound, and so also doubles the bandwidth used. Thus, on a phone line, when transmission goes beyond a certain speed, the sounds will be distorted because they go beyond the frequencies detectable by the human ear, the standard for which the telephone system was developed.

TELEPHONE LINES AND TELEPHONE LINKAGES

The great advantage of the public telephone network for data transmission is its widespread availability. There are telephones virtually everywhere, and wherever there is a telephone, a data transmission device can be connected to the line. However, since the phone system was originally designed to transmit the continuous frequencies of the human voice, it uses an analog signal, necessitating the use of modems or other devices to transmit digital data.

There are three common methods of establishing a telephone linkage between a terminal and a computer: dial access, use of a leased line between a single terminal and the computer, and the sharing of a leased line among a number of terminals on the same computer, using multiplexing techniques. Multiplexing is discussed in the section on data communications hardware later in this chapter.

Dial Access

The dial-access or dial-up approach enables regular telephone installations to be used for data transmission. The telephone line can still be used for voice communication when not in use for data transmission. Dial access also gives great flexibility. Different machines, perhaps offering quite different facilities, can be linked to one terminal at different times. A terminal used to charge a book may at another time be connected to a remote data base and at still another time may dial into the data base of a nearby library.

Dial access is cost-effective for situations where a specific terminal-computer linkage is of relatively short and infrequent duration—entailing only a few dozen transactions a day. (In an environment where a number of terminals need to access the computer on such a basis, it is possible to have more than one terminal assigned to a single computer port or input channel, thus reducing the cost of the computer installation.) The efficiency of dial access, however, is reduced by the same limitations that apply to regular telephone traffic—peak period loads that make connections difficult to establish—and by the restricted transmission speeds for data transmission over phone lines.

Until recently, a major advantage of using dial-up telephone facilities for terminal-computer linkage was economic. Most such installations are within local areas where relatively short distances are involved and local calling rates apply. However, this situation is changing as telephone companies revise their pricing structure and charge business and institutional users by the minute for local telephone calls. Costs are expected to rise further as local rates are restructured to absorb the loss of revenue from long-distance traffic attendant upon the restructuring of telephone company operations.

Certain technical aspects of dial-access linkage limit the extent to which techniques to increase the speed of data communications—and thus lower the costs—can be applied. Transmission speed, which is usually expressed in "baud" (one baud is one signal element per second), is a major factor. With voice-grade telephone lines and regular modems, the practical upper limit is 1800 baud. Higher speed modems are available that achieve faster data transmission by encoding more data bits in a baud. For example, a modem operating at 1200 baud, but encoding two bits in a baud, effectively transmits data at 2400 bits per second (bps). Some modems will transmit data over voice-grade lines at 4800 and 9600 bps. A penalty is paid for the very high speed in increased error rates and modem costs. Consequently, it is common to limit transmission speeds over voice lines to 4800 bits per second. Unfortunately, dumb terminals mandate the use of a special type of full-duplex modem in dial-up mode, effectively limiting transmission to 1200 bps. (Full-duplex is described later in this chapter.)

Leased Lines

All dial-up telephone service is publicly switched. In other words, the lines are switched through public exchanges (central telephone offices) to make temporary connections. Alternatively, a leased or dedicated line can be used to establish a permanent connection between computer devices.

A leased line between points sharing the same telephone exchange may be permanently connected via the local telephone switching office, but it would not be connected to the switch gear and signaling devices of that office. On the other hand, a link between more remote points would require a leased connection between telephone exchange offices that would use the same physical links as the switched circuits. It would not, however, have to carry the signaling that is needed on a switched line. Although in some parts of the United States phone companies offer Dataphone Digital Service (DDS) as an alternative to voice-grade lines, most leased lines are voice-grade. With present tariffs, there are virtually no cost savings to be realized through using DDS, even though modems are not required on equipment attached to such lines. However, DDS lines do offer greater reliability and better performance.

Just as one can have a telephone connection permanently wired, so it is with other types of lines. Telegraph lines, for example, which have a much lower speed of transmission than is possible over telephone lines, may be permanently connected. They may also be dialed like a telephone line, using a switched public network. Telex is similar; it exists throughout most of the world and permits transmission at 50 bits per second. Telex users can set up international connections to other countries. Some countries also have a switched public network that operates at a somewhat higher speed than Telex, but at lower speed than the telephone lines. In the United States, the TWX network offers speeds up to 150 bits per second. All of these communications lines are designated "sub-voice grade" because they are slower than telephone lines.

Advantages of Leased Lines

The cost of leased lines in mid-1983 varies from $7 to $14 per month per mile, but it can be expected to rise dramatically in the next few years. Even so, given the changes in dial-access pricing structures and the number of transactions per remote terminal per day (300 or more), most libraries can justify leasing a line. There are some real advantages in using leased lines that are permanently connected.

• If it is to be used for more than a given number of hours per day, the leased line is less expensive than the switched line. The "break-even point" varies depending on actual charges, which, in turn, depend on the mileage of the circuit. It may be as little as one hour or as much as several hours connect time per day.

• Leased lines can be specially treated or "conditioned" to compensate for the distortion they exhibit. Through conditioning, the number of data errors can be reduced or, alternatively, a higher transmission rate can be achieved. (Conditioning is discussed in more detail in the next section.) The switched connection, on the other hand, cannot be conditioned beforehand, because it is not known what path the circuit will take. A switched link established when dialing on one occasion is likely to follow a quite different physical path from that obtained by dialing at another time, and there are a large number of possible paths. Modems are now available that condition dynamically; that is, they can adjust to whatever connection they are used on. These devices enable higher speeds to be obtained, but they are expensive.

• Conditioned leased lines can often transmit data at a higher rate. Switched voice lines usually carry telephone company signaling within the bandwidth that can be used for data. Consequently, data transmission machines must be designed so that the data do not interfere with the common carrier's signaling. With some machines, this also makes the capacity available for data transmission somewhat less than that over a leased line. A common rate over a switched line in the 1960s was 1200 bits per second, whereas 2400 bits per second was common over a specially conditioned leased line. Because of improved modem designs, it is probable that in the mid-1980s speeds of 3600 bits per second over switched lines and 9600 bits per second over conditioned leased lines will become common. Already some modems transmit at higher speeds than 3600 bits per second over public voice-grade lines.

Line Conditioning

As explained above, leased voice-grade lines can be conditioned to improve their data transmission capabilities. The tariffs, or publicly approved pricing schedules, of the telephone companies—discussed later in this chapter—specify maximum allowable levels for certain types of distortion. An additional charge is made by most carriers for lines that are conditioned.

Ideally, a line for data transmission would have an equal drop or attenuation in signal voltage for all frequencies transmitted. Also, all frequencies would have the same propagation time, or signal delay. This is not so in practice. Different frequencies suffer different attenuation and different signal delay. Conditioning attempts to equalize the attenuation and delay at different frequencies. Standards are laid down in the tariffs for the measure of equalization that must be achieved.

The American Telephone and Telegraph Company, for example, has three types of conditioning in common use for voice lines carrying data, referred to as types C1, C2 and C4. The signal attenuation and delay at different frequencies must lie within certain limits for each type.

SIMPLEX, HALF-DUPLEX AND FULL-DUPLEX LINES

In designing a data communications system, it is necessary to decide whether a line must transmit in one direction only or in both directions. If the latter, it must also be decided whether the machines will transmit in both directions at the same time or alternately. Transmission lines are accordingly classed as simplex, half-duplex and full-duplex. In North America, these terms have the following meanings:

- Simplex lines transmit in one direction only.

- Half-duplex lines can transmit in either direction, but in only one direction at a time.

- Full-duplex lines transmit in both directions at once.

Thus, one full-duplex line is equivalent to two simplex or half-duplex lines used in opposite directions. The full-duplex line is sometimes referred to simply as "duplex." For full-duplex transmission, two channels are used, one transmitting in each direction. If data are relayed in a half-duplex mode, there must be a pause at the end of a transmission and a reversal in line before a reply can be transmitted and received. The delay, during which the direction of the transmission is reversed, is called the line turnaround time.

Simplex or half-duplex data transmission requires two wires to complete an electrical circuit. Usually a four-wire circuit is needed for full-duplex transmission. There is, however, an ingenious way to build what is in effect a four-wire circuit out of two wires: the bandwidth of the lines is split up into two separate frequency bands, one of which is used for transmission in one direction and the other for transmission in the opposite direction. This is referred to as line splitting and produces the equivalent of a four-wire circuit using only two wires. This approach permits full-duplex operation on two-wire circuits. Data transmission machines often have specifications saying whether they require a two-wire or four-wire circuit.

The preceding meanings of the words "simplex" and "half-duplex" are in current use in most of the world's computer industry and in the North American telecommunications industry. Throughout this book these terms are used with these meanings. However, the reader should be aware that the International Telecommunications Union, an organization that has determined most of the world's standards in telecommunications, defines them differently:

• Simplex lines permit the transmission of signals in either direction but not simultaneously.

• Half-duplex lines are designed for duplex operation but, because of the nature of the terminal equipment, they can be operated alternately only.

Thus, European telecommunications engineers use the terms differently than do computer manufacturers, most of which are North American.

Public telephone lines in North America are half-duplex. It is only with leased telephone lines that the user has a choice between half-duplex and full-duplex. In North America simplex lines are not generally used in data transmission because even if information is being sent in only one direction, control signals are normally sent back to the transmitting machine to tell it that the receiving machine is ready or is receiving the data correctly. As a rule, error signals (positive or negative acknowledgment) are sent back so that messages damaged by communication line errors can be retransmitted.

Many data transmission links use half-duplex lines, thus allowing the movement of transmittal control signals and the occurrence of two-way "conversational" transmissions. On some systems full-duplex lines provide more efficient use of the lines at little extra line cost—about 10% more. However, data transmission machines that can take advantage of full-duplex lines are more expensive than those that use half-duplex lines. Half-duplex transmission is, therefore, more common at present, although this situation might well change.

TARIFFS

The services offered by a telecommunications company are described in tariffs. A tariff is a document that (in the United States) is required by the regulating bodies that control the carriers. It specifies details of the service and its cost. The United States Federal Communications Commission (FCC) must eventually approve all interstate facilities, and similar state commissions control those within state boundaries. By law, all tariffs must be registered with these bodies. In most other countries, the telecommunications facilities are set up by government bodies and thus are directly under their control. A library should determine the tariffs that apply before planning its telecommunications network.

DATA COMMUNICATIONS HARDWARE

Normally, libraries purchase data communications hardware from the same source that provides other computing hardware. Thus, it is usually part of a turnkey system. However, it is possible to deal with a firm specializing in data communications. In that case, one must be careful that all hardware will be compatible. This section describes the data communications hardware required.

Modems and Data Sets

As previously noted, many of the communications lines over which data are to be sent are designed for analog transmission, not digital. If computer data are to be sent over such analog lines, the digital bit stream must be converted into an analog signal, using a modem or data set.

A modem converts the square-edged bit stream that leaves the computer (shown in Figure 4.1) into a range of frequencies suitable for transmitting over the analog communication line; then, at the other end of the line, a similar modem converts this range of frequencies back into a bit stream that replicates the original data stream. The modem tailors the signal to fit without undue distortion into the range of frequencies that the communication line handles. A pair of modems usually costs $1000 or less.

Most telegraph lines, other wideband lines of higher capacity than telephone lines, including cable, and most of the microwave radio links spanning North America are analog. These links, therefore, must also employ modems when they transmit digital signals. If microwave links or any other communication facility were designed specifically for data transmission, as may well happen in the future, they would be digital in operation, with digital repeaters, and thus would not require modems.

Multiplexors

Terminals located in groups at remote sites may be "multiplexed" as a single line using a multiplexor, a type of data terminal equipment designed to combine the transmissions of multiple terminals into one composite signal. Several terminals may be connected to a single multiplexor, and at the other end of the line over which the signal is transmitted, an identical multiplexor separates and reconstitutes the original input from each terminal. In the case of a minicomputer, the equipment routes the signals to the appropriate ports of the computer or to yet another multiplexor. Neither terminal equipment nor the computer hardware or software need to be changed when multiplexing is undertaken. Either dial-up or leased lines may be used with multiplexors.

There are several multiplexing techniques; statistical multiplexing is usually the most cost-effective. A statistical multiplexor uses a small microprocessor and a buffer memory so that data can be stored temporarily during periods of peak activity. This permits more terminals to share a line because the "stat mux," as it is often called, smooths out the traffic flow. It allocates the shared line in such a way that up to eight terminals, each operating at 1200 bps, can share a single 1200 baud voice-grade telephone line transmitting at 2400 bps. Very high capacity stat muxes are called "data concentrators."

Stat muxes typically cost from $2500 to $10,000 each, depending upon the number of terminals they handle. Most models of multiplexors incorporate modems. A rule of thumb is to budget $2000 per terminal. The cost of data concentrators may go considerably higher, and the special modems they require may cost as much as $6000 a pair.

It is possible to network stat muxes or data concentrators. Figure 4.2 illustrates such a network. Several terminals at a branch library may share a multiplexor (MUX A) that is connected to another multiplexor (MUX B) through a pair of modems (M) and a phone line. In turn, the second multiplexor (MUX B) transmits the separated data streams to yet another multiplexor (MUX C). Several other terminals may also come into MUX C by phone lines or by direct wired links so that all share a single line to the central processor. The multiplexor (MUX D) at the central site then splits all the transmissions among the appropriate ports of the computer.

Concentrating terminals becomes advantageous when the costs of the individual telephone lines (if any) from the terminals to the multiplexors, the telecommunications hardware and the shared multiple line charges are added up and found to be less than the cost of the larger number of individual telephone lines and modems.

Multidrop Concentrators

Related to the data concentrator is the "multidrop concentrator." This recently introduced device makes it possible to use the multidrop concept described earlier in this chapter in the asynchronous communications environment of minicomputer-based systems. The multidrop concentrator allows a single telephone line to connect individual terminals or clusters of terminals at several points or nodes along the telephone line rather than just at each end. The multidrop concentrator at the central site, a processor, would poll or communicate with all of the node concentrators in round-robin fashion. Unlike the polling techniques used in synchronous communication for mainframe computers, intelligent terminals are not required. Thus, multidrop concentrators offer the economy of asynchronous hardware and the efficiency of multidropping on a single telecommunications line. The cost of a multidrop concentrator is $3500 or more, and the node concentrators cost up to $2500 each. Only very large libraries with concentrations of many terminals along a single axis should consider this technique.

Port Concentrators

Another related piece of telecommunications hardware is the port concentrator or intelligent port selector. It allows one computer port to communicate with several terminals, not just in dial-up situations, but also when leased lines are used. As a transmission comes

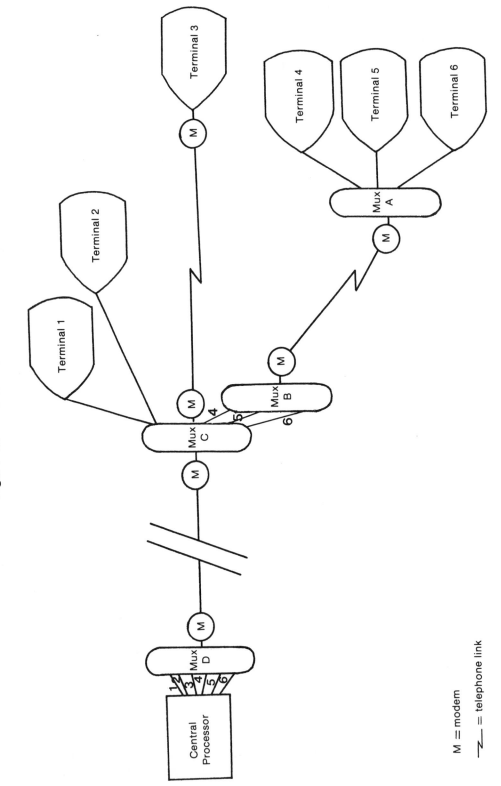

Figure 4.2: A "Stat Mux" Network

M = modem

∕ = telephone link

in, it is directed to any vacant port, rather than to a port pre-assigned to that particular terminal. Unlike the other multiplexing devices discussed, this device does require some changes in the computer system software. It therefore requires the full cooperation of the software supplier. Currently, no library software supplier places a high priority on providing this capability. Port concentrators typically cost more than $10,000.

EVALUATION OF CURRENT OPTIONS

Given the range of telecommunications options available to computer users and the expected increase in the number of suppliers of telecommunications hardware and transmission lines as the telephone industry is deregulated, librarians managing automated systems will need to periodically reexamine their telecommunications approaches to ensure that they continue to take advantage of the most cost-effective options available. The following rules of thumb are valid as of fall 1983:

• If the terminals are within 2000 feet of the computer, direct connections using line drivers are generally most cost-effective.

• When terminals are remote from the computer and widely scattered, direct connection through telephone lines with modems may be the best choice. Normally, dedicated leased lines are more cost-effective than dial-up lines when a library's telecommunications costs have been more than $1000 a month or have risen more than 20% in the past year.

• If the remote terminals are concentrated at a small number of sites, if there are more than 25 remote terminals or if telecommunications costs are more than $1500 per month, it is quite likely that the use of statistical multiplexing will be more cost-effective than leased lines using modems alone.

• If there are more than 50 remote terminals, it may be possible to network statistical multiplexors to realize even greater cost savings.

Some libraries may be able to reduce ongoing telecommunications costs by up to 90% by investing in telecommunications hardware. The "payback" period—the time required to recover the capital outlay for telecommunications hardware—may be as short as two to three years.

While a library may wish to have the vendor of its computer system review and modify its telecommunications, it is not mandatory that it do so. Virtually all telecommunications hardware requires no changes in software. A library may choose to retain an expert in telecommunications if its vendor does not appear to have appropriate expertise or if the vendor's prices for a telecommunications analysis are too high.

The vendor should be notified of planned changes in the telecommunications system as should the telephone company(ies). Despite frequent protests by vendors and telephone companies, they may not prohibit the linkage of telecommunications equipment purchased from other sources to their equipment.

CABLE FOR DATA TRANSMISSION

There has been considerable interest in the use of cable systems for data transmission. As with telephone lines, cables can be used to transmit data exclusively or intermingled with analog audio/video information.

Cable as a data communications medium offers high capacity, speed and relatively widespread availability. However, to install a cable system specifically and solely to link a number of sites that wish to exchange digital data is prohibitively expensive except in very localized high-data-volume situations. An example of this use of cable is New York City, where Manhattan Cable provides cable-based data communications to 200 high-volume banking and financial customers through an installation of only 17 miles of communications cable. Each account contributes at least $200,000 a year to Manhattan Cable's revenue. Such a company is unlikely to be interested in servicing libraries, which have comparatively low volumes of data to be transmitted.

The secret to cost reduction in low-volume use of cable is to piggy-back the data communications on an existing service such as the systems installed for cable television. Such use of the medium has the potential to reduce the costs of current telephone-based communications by 10% to 40%, but there is not yet enough experience to permit judgment of whether or not cable is a viable alternative in practice.

There are other constraints. Data communication to link terminals and/or computers requires a medium capable of two-way (interactive) communication. At the simplest level, a terminal operator needs to transmit a search request and be able to receive the results of the search or to transmit a message requesting that an item be placed on hold and to receive confirmation that the message has been received. In practical economic terms, such capabilities are only available on cable television systems that have been designed as two-way systems. Only 1% of the U.S. communities with cable television have such two-way services. Even in installations with this capability, library use of a cable channel for data communications requires that the system have spare channels not currently devoted to other applications. The majority of installed systems do not have spare capacity, although most recently awarded franchises do have a number of unused channels.

Should a library be in a situation in which both of these requirements—two-way capability and channel availability—are met, the way is still not clear for the use of cable as a data communications medium. That is because most cable companies are not yet interested in supporting data communication. Factors such as company priorities and economics will be keystones in determining the future of the medium. Until cable companies are convinced data communication will be profitable and within their technical capacities, little will happen.

While cable has the potential to offer better and cheaper channels for data transfer, quality control can also be a problem—some systems do not perform any better than telephone linkages. As of fall 1983 no library in the United States is using cable as an operational system for data delivery. Several, however, have plans to do so: the Pikes Peak (Colorado Springs, CO), Columbus (OH), New Orleans, Iowa City and Atlanta public libraries.

The thinking on the design of data communications systems is changing. No longer are such networks seen as being composed of one communications medium; development is moving toward a multi-media approach which combines cable, telephone, local area networks, etc. Other emerging data transmission alternatives include satellites, which are cost-effective for distances in excess of 700 miles; digital telephone facilities; microwave for local data transmission; and local area networks, which are *very* local, generally facilitating linkages within a building or between adjacent buildings. Implementation of multi-media data linkages is likely to be hampered by FCC regulations, which require that data communications applications using media other than the telephone lines be licensed.

To keep abreast of future developments in this area, library managers should maintain an awareness of developments in data communications for the general market. They should also follow the progress of the public libraries named above that plan to use cable for data communications.

SUMMARY

The growth of automation in libraries has resulted in increasing reliance on remote terminals linked to computers and on the transmitting of information between computer systems. Because of its virtually universal availability, the telephone system is likely to continue to be the principal medium for data communications despite limitations in bandwidth and the need to convert computer data's digital signal to an analog signal for transmission. The growth of cable systems may result in greater use of this medium for data communications. However, most existing systems do not offer interactive capabilities, and it is not clear that cable companies will want to support data communications.

A number of options exist for establishing phone line links—including dial-up access and the use of leased lines or multiplexed leased lines. Direct hardwiring of terminals that are located near the host computer is also possible. Choosing among these requires a careful evaluation of anticipated use and costs, including the costs of different types of hardware used for different links. Because both use and costs are unlikely to remain fixed, the library manager should reexamine the options from time to time.

Considerations involved in building the library's data base are the subject of Chapter 5.

5

The Data Base

Fundamental to any automation project is the creation of a data base of machine-readable records, both for the bibliographic items in the library collection and for library patron data if circulation is to be automated. Bibliographic records are the more difficult and costly to create; it is wise to budget $1.00 per record. Consultants and vendors usually recommend that libraries with fewer than 500,000 volumes have machine-readable records for at least 50% of their holdings before installing a computer system. Larger libraries should have machine-readable records for at least the past five years' acquisitions.

Before describing the creation of machine-readable records, it is necessary to discuss the importance of standards and the nature of the data base.

STANDARDS

More and more, libraries do not automate in isolation. Often two or more libraries share a single system. Others procure separate systems but include the potential for dial-up access into one another's computers for sharing information or interlibrary loan. In all these cases, compatibility is important. Thus, the libraries' objective is to foster compatibility among their files of machine-readable bibliographic records; this cannot be achieved unless the libraries agree to adopt a uniform set of standards for recording the data. Two levels of standards are required: the first, to govern the rules for transcribing the data; the second, to prescribe the way in which these data will be encoded in machine-readable form. The combination and sharing of the files will be further facilitated if the libraries also agree to develop records that contain the same level of detail.

Standards for Bibliographic Description

The success of bibliographic utilities—shown by the fact that so many libraries are prepared to rely on cataloging performed by other libraries—is due in large part to their enforcement of cataloging standards supported by the majority of North American libraries. These standards, which apply to the transcription of data, govern the quality of the cataloging. The same standards have also facilitated the success of nonautomated shared cataloging schemes, such as the Library of Congress Catalog Card Service.

Primary among these standards are the Anglo-American Cataloging Rules, which govern the selection and presentation of information in a catalog entry and prescribe the way in which variant factors such as corporate and personal names are to be consistently cited. Equally important is the use of standard subject and classification schemes—such as the Library of Congress Subject Headings List and Sears List of Subject Headings, and the Library of Congress and Dewey Decimal Classification Schemes—which ensure acceptable consistency in these parts of the catalog record. Libraries must adhere to these standards in order to minimize the number of expensive changes needed before they can use the standard records in their own internal systems, manual or automated. Only in this way can they receive the full benefits of accessing shared bibliographic files.

Standards for Encoding Data in Machine-readable Form

With the widespread use of machine-readable records, the second level of standardization—formats and guidelines for encoding the catalog data in machine-readable form—has become essential. In addition to supporting cost efficiency in in-house automated systems, the adoption of a standard bibliographic format for encoding data in machine-readable form is required if information is to be exchanged among several systems.

The standard bibliographic format is MARC (MAchine Readable Cataloging). Use of the MARC standard allows any system to output a MARC record and any to receive it. This standardization is basic to the future of resource sharing locally, statewide, regionally and nationally.

Use of the MARC standard also has benefits for libraries that undertake little exchange of data with other libraries. Every bibliographic utility, turnkey vendor, jobber and commercial bibliographic service supports MARC and can provide output and accept input in this format. A library can, therefore, load records from any of these sources into its system, and it can have tapes from its system loaded by these service organizations without reformatting. For example, computer output microform (COM) catalogs can be produced without extensive preprocessing. A library using MARC can also move data through electronic interfaces without having to introduce an additional reformatting step. Reformatting can be expensive: service bureaus usually level a charge of $.05 to $.25 per record for reformatting when this is required before the record can be used.

The introduction of the MARC format will initially make cataloging slower because it involves the recording of information often not included in traditional or manual cataloging. However, within a few months cataloging productivity should increase. The increase will be significantly above the levels achieved under manual cataloging if the adoption of the format is accompanied by the introduction of an automated cataloging support system that draws on the resources of a bibliographic utility's data base.

In 1981 D. Kaye Gapen, then Assistant Director for Technical Services at Iowa State University and now Director of Libraries at the University of Alabama, was commissioned by the Association of Research Libraries Task Force on Bibliographic Control to prepare a paper on the feasibility and consequences of simplifying the MARC formats. Ms. Gapen found that simplification of the formats was not necessarily feasible: substantial costs would result from revising the formats even to simplify them; and, once mastered, like other cataloging rules and standards, the formats did not hamper cataloging efficiency. In addition, the variety of products generated from machine-readable records necessitates the retention of many format elements. Ms. Gapen concluded that rather than deleting elements, the Association and other interested groups should seek consistency in the formats for all types of material and should encourage consistent implementation of the formats by all of the major agencies involved in the formulation and distribution of bibliographic records.[1]

LEVEL OF DETAIL

A library adminstration may decide to develop records that adhere to the accepted bibliographic and format standards, yet fear that the expense of developing and storing records that contain the full level of detail supported by these standards will be prohibitive. An examination of the development of automated library applications and computer hardware strongly supports the wisdom of building a data base containing full bibliographic records.

Full Bibliographic Records

Libraries that automated in the early 1970s built bibliographic records averaging fewer than 120 characters each, just sufficient for the author's name, a truncated title and the call number. The high cost of storage on mainframe-based systems and the limited secondary storage capacity of minicomputer-based systems forced this decision. The first turnkey circulation system had two disk drives with a total of 20MB of storage, enough for only 100,000 very brief bibliographic records. Since most of the automation in the early 1970s involved acquisitions or circulation, the brief records did not pose a serious problem for libraries.

By the mid-1970s, most libraries with automated systems were loading records of 300 to 400 characters. Storage costs had dropped, capacity had increased, and terminals to circulation systems were beginning to be installed at reference desks to facilitate public service staff queries of the online data base.

By 1980 disk drives of 300MB capacity were available. Some minicomputers could accommodate eight disk drives for a total of 2.4 billion characters of storage. Libraries were beginning to think about the future adoption of online or patron access catalogs with provision for sophisticated Boolean searching. It became obvious that full bibliographic records would be desirable. Fortunately, not only had storage capacities increased, but prices had dropped so that a 300MB disk drive cost no more in 1980 than a 30MB unit had five years before.

In 1983, because the unit cost drops dramatically as the size of the secondary storage unit increases, the cost of a 300MB drive is actually less than twice that of a 60MB drive. The extra cost of storing a 700 character full bibliographic record is, therefore, minimal. On the other hand, the cost of expanding a 300 or 400 character record to a 700 character record is significant—usually at least $.15 per record if the record is in the MARC communications format and can be matched to a full-MARC data base with a minimum of human intervention. It is now substantially less expensive to purchase the capacity to load a full bibliographic record than to obtain a smaller capacity and pay for a storage upgrade and a record expansion later.

A data base with full-length records averaging 700 characters can be used to display either full records or brief records for library users. Many libraries prefer to have a patron at a terminal get only a brief record on a first search. However, full records are necessary to support Boolean searching so that users can sift through many records to identify those most relevant to their needs. For example, a person at a terminal may enter two or more subject descriptors, a year before which citations are not wanted, the stipulation that works should be retrieved only if written in one of several specified languages and a requirement that the item include a bibliography.

Should a library, nevertheless, decide that it is going to use brief records, it should at least adhere to the MARC format and use MARC tags so that searches begun on one library system can be continued on another system using the same bibliographic record structure.

Long-term Financial Implications

A data base is the most important part of an automated library system. While hardware may be replaced from time to time (the norm is every five to seven years) and software is periodically rewritten to transfer it to other hardware, to improve its performance or to enhance it, the bibliographic files, if well done, will outlast several generations of hardware and software.

The machine-readable bibliographic file is analogous to the 100% rag catalog cards that libraries have been filing in their card catalogs. The cards are intended to last indefinitely and to be transferred to new card catalog cabinets when the old cabinets are replaced. Similarly, the bibliographic file represents a considerable investment and should be of high quality and transferable. A few libraries have used the same MARC records on three computer systems over a period of 13 years.

Should the MARC standard be revised, the cost of changing records that have been created in conformity to the MARC format should be low because machine methods would almost certainly be available for the conversion from the old standard to the new standard. Each user of records in the standard format would bear only a small part of the cost of writing the conversion programs. The conversion of nonstandard files requires special conversion programs that must be charged to a single library. Similarly, as was evident in the recent change in the Anglo-American Cataloging Rules, libraries with records encoded in the standard format and constructed according to the rules governing bibliographic description can also weather changes in these standards more economically because they can use the product of shared conversion projects.

RETROSPECTIVE CONVERSION

The most popular method of creating a local data base is to use the archival tapes generated by Online Computer Library Center, Inc. (OCLC), Research Libraries Information Network (RLIN), Washington Library Network (WLN) or University of Toronto Library Automation Systems (UTLAS) as part of a library's current cataloging activity. Machine-readable records in the MARC communications format can be processed into an operating format and loaded into the turnkey system. Every computer system requires that records be organized in an operating format. Initially, each system had a unique format, but there is now a trend to standardization. In fact, as of early 1983, most turnkey systems used the MARC communications format as the operating format. As noted above, all major turnkey vendors are now able to accept MARC-formatted records directly into their systems without requiring any external reformatting. OCLC, whose services are described in a later section, is the most widely used source of bibliographic records.

Alternative Conversion Methods

Most libraries have only a small percentage of their titles on their bibliographic utility archival tapes. Retrospective conversion is, therefore, necessary to create a data base comprehensive enough to support a circulation system or an online catalog. It was the practice until the mid-1970s to convert "on-the-fly." Brief records for circulation control were keyed in when the material was charged out or returned. In this way time was not expended on the conversion of records for materials that were not being circulated. The move toward fuller bibliographic records forced a change in the approach.

Using a Service Bureau

The most popular method in the latter part of the 1970s became the keying of the International Standard Book Number (ISBN), the Library of Congress Card Number (LCCN), and brief author and title data on magnetic tape and the dispatch of these brief records to a service bureau for matching against a full-MARC data base. The service bureau was typically a firm that performed commercial cataloging or COM catalog production services (for example, Baker & Taylor Co., Blackwell North America Inc., Auto-Graphics, Inc. and Science Press). The firm would create a file of "hits"—all MARC records that appeared to match the library's records—and send a printout of it to the library for review and correction. The approach was quite labor intensive and normally cost the library at least $1.25 to $1.50 per record. Concurrently with creating the proof list, the vendor could produce another list of the entries not found in the machine-readable data base. For these non-matches full bibliographic entries would then have to be created and keyed by the library staff. In this approach, the "hit rate" for academic libraries tended to be low because the vendors' data bases, which usually consisted only of MARC tapes and the original cataloging of some previous customers, usually public libraries, were not good matches for academic collections.

Another method has been to use an existing circulation system data base of brief records to match against the vendor's data base. The same process as described for the brief record keying approach is followed. Labor costs are slightly lower because no original keying has to be undertaken.

Carrollton Press, Inc. offers a retrospective conversion service based on the keying of brief records onto floppy disks using a microcomputer provided by the vendor. The disks are reformatted onto tape and matched against both the MARC and REMARC data bases maintained by Carrollton Press.* In 1983 the rate charged was $.20 for matching against a MARC record and $.50 for matching against a REMARC record. The library incurs not only the labor cost of entering the brief search keys but also the cost of reviewing the "hits" identified in the matching. The average total cost is probably less than $1.00 per record, including vendor charges and labor.

Using a Leased Generalized Data Base

Yet another alternative for libraries that have already installed a minicomputer is to load a generalized data base of MARC records and bibliographic records from other libraries. The source for this data base is usually one of the service bureaus mentioned previously. Random sampling should be used to determine that the data base includes a majority of the library's holdings. Loading these entries into the library's minicomputer avoids any typing and eliminates vendor matching. The immediate review of matches at the terminal is faster than searching printouts. Such use of a minicomputer is feasible because of the large data storage capacity that is now available.

By loading a leased generalized data base on a minicomputer in the library, all steps described in the first alternative for conversion can be achieved simultaneously. Books are brought to a terminal and records are retrieved by ISBN, LCCN or, if they cannot be found, by an author/title search. The item number labels are attached to the book and are recorded in the data base along with other information needed in the item file—for example, location. The items not found in the data base can be cataloged directly from the title pages as the books are handled. The entire conversion process can thus be completed at one time.

While total labor costs may be $.90 or less per record, this approach to retrospective conversion does require significant computer capacity for the heavy processing load. Thus, to use this method, a library must plan its computer system accordingly, as the Tacoma (WA) Public Library—apparently the first to use this conversion method—learned the hard way. In 1978 the library installed a minicomputer only large enough to support its projected circulation system. The loading of the temporary data base and the creation of the parallel institutional data base used all the disk storage; the impact of 20 terminal operators engaged in systematic data base building degraded response time to more than one minute.

---

*Carrollton Press is the firm responsible for retrospective conversion of more than 5 million pre-1968 Library of Congress records, a project known as REMARC.

Using an Institutional Mainframe Computer

Librarians sometimes ask whether retrospective conversion could not be undertaken using an existing institutional mainframe computer. Unfortunately, special software is required, and the only software packages known to be suitable (such as DOBIS and NOTIS, which are described in Chapter 6) cost in excess of $70,000.

Using a Commercial Data Entry Service

A few libraries have had their shelflists keyed by commercial data entry services, such as Scantech. The services typically charge $1.95 per thousand characters or $1.40 per full bibliographic record. That approach is particularly popular among libraries that do not use a bibliographic utility for shared cataloging and thus do not have access to an online data base.

Commercial keying services, such as Electronic Keying, Inc. (EKI), that have done retrospective conversions for libraries by keying full bibliographic records from a shelflist for $2.00 to $6.00 per record, including editing and authority control, now offer a less expensive service. A library can provide LCCNs and local call number and holdings information, and the firms will have LCCNs matched against the MARC tapes of a major service bureau and add the other information when records are found. The price of a magnetic tape of all matching records in mid-1983 is around $.30 per hit, including the addition of the local call number and holdings. The hit rate for medium-sized public libraries has been 60% to 70%. There is too little experience with academic libraries to estimate a hit rate, but it would presumably be lower than the hit rate realized by medium-sized public libraries and substantially less than the 80%-90% that academic libraries could expect using the OCLC data base.

Such firms will also match brief records (100 to 130 characters) against the MARC data base, extract matches and add local information for approximately $.60 per record.

The OCLC Program

Libraries that participate in the OCLC shared cataloging program have virtually all opted to use the OCLC online retrospective conversion program. Operators merely enter the ISBN, LCCN or author/title key and retrieve an OCLC record, much as they do in the case of regular cataloging. The regular FTU (first-time-use) charge is waived and a lower retrospective conversion rate is charged. The rate as of August 1983 is $.90 per record during peak system use hours and $.22 during off-peak hours. The total cost of such retrospective conversion has been estimated at $.89 per record. This is the lowest cost retrospective conversion approach available at the time of this writing.

Many libraries lack the staff and the OCLC terminals to undertake this type of retrospective conversion program, despite the attractive price. For them OCLC offers a retrospective conversion service. The rate quoted in 1983 was $.75 to $1.50 per record depending upon a number of factors: the number of records, the number of titles to be converted by type of materials (i.e., monographs, serials, etc.), the number of titles to be converted by language, the percentage of titles requiring original input (expected hit rate against the OCLC data base), the percentage of titles that have LCCN or other unique search keys, the amount of editing of matching records desired by the contracting institution and the amount of local data to be entered.

Commercial firms, such as ProLibra, Inc., that have arranged after-hours access to OCLC terminals in libraries began to offer retrospective conversion services using the OCLC system in late 1982. The firms act strictly as a library's agent and use the library's account number. They build a data base that will be for the exclusive use of the client library. The cost per record may be $1.00 or more. If libraries choose to convert most records internally and leave the difficult conversion to be done by such a firm, the per record charge can be substantially higher.

USING THE RECORDS IN A LOCAL SYSTEM

The goal of creating a data base—whether of bibliographic or patron records—is to use it in a computer system that automates library services. Both types of records may require special editing to meet the library's needs.

Bibliographic Records

Most of the machine-readable bibliographic records created in a retrospective conversion project will at some time in the future be loaded into a local system, usually a turnkey system. Turnkey vendors provide a number of services to assist libraries with this process.

Vendors usually agree to manage any necessary reformatting and loading of existing machine-readable bibliographic records into the systems they supply. Most systems have been designed to accommodate a variety of conversion methods to ensure that a library can begin using the system quickly and without large conversion expenditures. This is almost always accomplished by adopting MARC as the internal operating format or by having built-in conversion programs to translate MARC into the internal operating format of the system.

The turnkey system vendor also assigns an installation specialist to assist in the overall implementation of the system. One of the responsibilities of this person is to help the library develop a file building strategy. If MARC records are available, the following strategy is generally adopted.

Loading and Reformatting MARC Records

First, the library loads bibliographic data from magnetic tapes supplied by the bibliographic utility (e.g., OCLC) or by commercial vendors who follow the MARC format. The system automatically stores the MARC records online and reformats the data into the end-user format specified by the library—the format to be displayed on the terminal screen. The end-user format is referred to as the presentation or display record. It differs from the MARC record in that it does not show the tags and it may have some fields removed.

When the library, working with the vendor's representative, has determined the criteria for reformatting the title information and the tape has been loaded, the system stores the MARC bibliographic data on a magnetic disk. The library may then preview the information as it would appear after reformatting, before storing it in the appropriate system files. If the format is not correct, the library may modify the specifications for formatting and have the system reformat the MARC records again. Once the library approves the end-user format, the system stores the information in both the MARC format and the display format.

The practice of turnkey vendors is to go through the MARC format field by field to determine which elements of the MARC record are to be loaded into the system for retention and which are to be displayed.

However, a library loading records into a computer system should realize that not all systems offer the option of maintaining both a MARC record file and a display format file. With some systems, deletion of a tag or portion thereof will not only eliminate the tag from the display, but will also eliminate it from the record file; that is, the information will not be stored in the system.

If the library subscribes to bibliographic utility tapes on a regular basis, they may be used to maintain the system's bibliographic files on an ongoing basis using this same approach.

Loading and Reformatting Non-MARC Records

Turnkey vendors also assist libraries in transferring bibliographic records in non-MARC formats to their systems. If machine-readable data are available in any format (e.g., COM catalog records, book catalog records, punched cards, etc.) the vendor will arrange for the data to be reformatted to the library's specifications and loaded into the system's bibliographic file. This is usually done by the turnkey vendor's contracting with a service bureau such as Auto-Graphics, Blackwell North America or Brodart, Inc. to match the records against a MARC bibliographic resource file.

Keying in Records

Many libraries have created and continue to maintain their own bibliographic files by keying both title and item record data on the system's terminals. This is a labor-intensive procedure, but vendors have designed a number of helpful features in their file maintenance programs to make this conversion method as easy and efficient as possible. For example, the programs incorporate a search of the files at the time of entry and notify the operator immediately if a similar record is already in the file. Since updating the file is done immediately, there is virtually no possibility that the same record will inadvertently be entered twice.

Once input, the entire record may be recalled online. The library determines the display level for all system processes and inquiry through the system software, dictating when the complete record is shown and when only part of the record is displayed. Any specific field in the record may be edited without reentry of the whole record through the program.

Vendors' File Maintenance Programs

The typical vendor's file maintenance software includes a wide variety of functions. Using this program it is possible to:

- Add a record

- Add an item to a record

- Add a volume to a multi-volume work

- Change a field

- Change an access key

- Merge two or more records

- Duplicate a record and rename it from one key to another

- Delete a volume

- Delete an item

Rapid keying is facilitated by special interactive dialogs. For example, the title template feature of most systems enables libraries to create a new title record by copying data from a similar title record already on file, thus reducing the amount of keying required. All such file maintenance dialogs have been designed to minimize the amount of keying required, allowing for rapid input of title, item and patron records, while simultaneously assuring verification and data integrity and reducing the possibility of operator error.

Authority File Records

Almost all vendors make it possible to load tapes of authority records, but software to manipulate the records is limited. A library can also create a file of authority records by entering the records at a terminal one at a time. Once the records are loaded, the file is available for searching, but in the current design of most turnkey systems it cannot be electronically linked to the bibliographic file. Changes in the authority file and the bibliographical file must, therefore, be made separately. The linkage of these two files, called online authority control, is expected to be generally available by mid-1985.

Copy-specific Data

Turnkey vendor software includes provision for the entry of copy-specific or item information by tape loading or by keying at a terminal. Many libraries' bibliographic records contain some copy-specific information. If so, it can be stripped from the bibliographic record and placed in the item file by having the vendor write software for that purpose. There is usually no charge if the bibliographic record is in the MARC format because the vendor will already have written the program for earlier customers. All information that is lacking will have to be added by keyboarding. A typical copy-specific file record has the following elements:

- Label number

- Local call number

- Short title (temporary cataloging)

- Material type

- Serial volume, part or date

- Acquisitions date

- Acquisitions price

- Current owning agency

- Location within agency

- Original owning agency

- Original location

- Loan period

- Date charged

- Date due

- Charge type

- Latest circulation date

- Cumulative circulation count

- Holds or reserves

- Notices

Not all of this information needs to be entered at the time the record is created; some of it is entered by the system when a transaction occurs. The information that is required in the initial copy record can be entered by bringing each item to a terminal and calling up the bibliographic record by entering a short search key. The system is then instructed to add the information to be entered to the copy-specific record linked with that bibliographic record. A skilled operator can enter up to 35 items per hour. Another approach is to have the system print out each bibliographic record on a separate slip of paper and then take these to the shelves to obtain the missing information for subsequent entry at a terminal.

While the latter approach saves bringing each book to the conversion area, it is more costly because each record has to be written and then keyed. The former approach involves only keying.

Patron File Creation

Turnkey systems provide for loading and maintenance of patron information using either the magnetic tape facility or online keyboard data entry. Libraries that have access to machine-readable records—such as faculty-student lists in an academic library or employee records in a special library—may transfer these data to the system by simple tape loading and performing a subsequent online edit. When reformatting is required, most turnkey vendors will provide the service for a fee.

Libraries that have no patron information in machine-readable form may add patron records to the system by keying at the terminals. Two approaches may be used to accomplish this task.

The library may choose to issue new patron cards. Before going online, the library verifies the patrons' data from existing or new patron registration forms and enters the records into the system by keying them. The system then prints a patron card for each name. The appropriate labels are attached to the cards, and the cards are filed in name order at the circulation desk awaiting pickup.

Alternatively, if the library maintains a patron registration file, it may attach labels to existing patron cards. Prior to going online, the library asks patrons coming into the library to verify their name and address data with the registration clerk. The registration cards are pulled from the file and checked by the patron for accuracy. At that time a label is attached to the patron's card, and a matching label is attached to the registration card, which is used as the source document. The applications are coded with the patron's statistical category. The information is then keyed into the system. The applications are not refiled but are kept in label-number order to be used for future verification.

The second approach minimizes delay for the patron, familiarizes the patron with the label before the system is actually in use for circulation and means that the cards and labels are not issued for inactive patrons. The activity can usually be handled by the registration clerk with no delay in checkout activity.

Vendors usually recommend that staff presently allocated to patron registration and overdues be used to enter patron information. The average rate for entry of patron information, based on the experience of some 500 libraries, is 50 records per hour.[2] This rate assumes that the operator is entering from a document containing name, address, phone number, bar code label and the appropriate statistical category assigned to that patron.

SUMMARY

Creation of an adequate and reliable data base is essential to the success of a library automation project. Although patron records may be structured to suit the needs of the individual library, there are important reasons to use standardized formats in the creation of machine-readable bibliographic records. Standards for bibliographic description make it possible for libraries to share cataloging and other information. Use of the MARC format for encoding bibliographic information allows libraries to convert records by matching against the data bases of other libraries or bibliographic services. Once the data base is built, the standardization of formats permits sharing of data or systems and facilitates searching among libraries.

Several options exist for converting bibliographic records to machine-readable form. Most popular is online retrospective conversion using the data base of a bibliographic utility. The second most frequently used method is keying in of brief records and matching them against the data base of a commercial service bureau. The former has the benefits of being completed in one step and having a high hit rate. The latter involves smaller payments to vendors but requires more in-house labor because the resulting vendor list must be reviewed. Also, for academic and special libraries, the hit rate is lower than could be expected from a bibliographic utility. Other alternatives include the use of a leased generalized data base and the use of commercial data entry services.

Turnkey systems include a number of services that assist libraries in loading bibliographic records. Both MARC and non-MARC records can be reformatted to meet the library's requirements. In addition, file maintenance programs allow for the updating of old records and adding of new records after the system has been installed. Most systems also allow for creation of authority file records and copy-specific records.

Turnkey systems also provide for patron record maintenance. The records themselves may be created by loading from lists available on magnetic tape or by online keyboard entry.

Chapter 6 discusses the current options in library automation and profiles the major turnkey vendors.

FOOTNOTES

1. D. Kaye Gapen, unpublished report to the Association of Research Libraries Task Force on Bibliographic Control, 1981.

2. Telephone conversation with representative of CL Systems, Inc., December 14, 1982.

6

Options for Automating

The library manager who seeks to undertake the automation of one or more functions in the 1980s is faced with more choices than ever before. Six major options are available:

- Acquiring a turnkey stand-alone system

- Purchasing a software package and using a stand-alone mini or mainframe computer

- Developing a system in-house

- Contracting for a commercial service

- Contracting with a bibliographic utility

- Relying on the data processing facilities and staff of the library's parent organization

Turnkey systems—those that include in the price all hardware, software, installation, training and ongoing support—have been by far the most popular. In fact, more than 85% of all libraries automating circulation (the most commonly automated function) have chosen this approach. However, any automation study should consider all available options, and examine their advantages and disadvantages.

This chapter will provide guidelines for evaluating the major options and will also examine the benefits and problems of sharing a system. It will note ways in which the library can protect itself from outgrowing a system and will discuss issues in the development of interfaces for connecting different systems. Profiles of leading turnkey vendors appear at the end of the chapter. Detailed features and costs of specific systems are not included, because these change very rapidly. Library managers should keep abreast of the latest developments by reading the periodical literature, scanning vendor information, attending professional conferences, at which new systems features are often introduced, and talking to colleagues in other libraries.

TURNKEY SYSTEMS

Turnkey systems are generally the most cost-effective and reliable option. As noted, the vendor supplies hardware, software, installation, training and ongoing support of both hardware and software. The software maintenance program also includes enhancements or improvements in capabilities. No electronic data processing expertise is required on the part of the library staff. There is usually a firm contract price and predictable delivery date. The library has total control over the computer, the peripheral equipment and the software. Because the system has frequently been installed and tested elsewhere, performance is usually reliable.

In mid-1983, there were six established turnkey vendors—Avatar, Inc.; CL Systems, Inc. (CLSI); CTI Library Systems, Inc.; DataPhase Systems, Inc.; Geac Canada Ltd.; and Universal Library Systems. All but Avatar have had sales of more than $2.5 million in the past two years and also have at least six installed systems. These vendors are discussed later in the chapter. In addition, there were several newcomers seeking accounts.

Each group had certain advantages. The established firms offered somewhat more mature software products and relatively low risk, while the newcomers offered their first customers the opportunity to shape system development. The first customer must be prepared for some problems, however. While the customer may have a fixed contract price, the cost of software development to the vendor may rise dramatically above projections. Development may take two years or more, and a vendor may choose to breach the contract rather than complete the work. The customer also has to be careful that its needs will continue to be supported once the vendor has several customers and begins to generalize the system to meet the needs of different sizes and types of libraries.

Most of the turnkey systems installed in libraries have been stand-alone online circulation systems, but since 1980 the trend has been toward integrated systems with several functions sharing a common bibliographic data base. These systems are maintained entirely on a minicomputer and do not rely on a larger computer for any part of the processing.

In 1982 CLSI began actively marketing a system configured around a powerful microcomputer, the PDP 11/23. This micro is quite different from the better known personal micros in that it can support several users accessing different functions at the same time. By mid-1983 four vendors—CLSI, Avatar, CTI and DataPhase—were offering micro-based integrated systems for as little as $40,000, and all but DataPhase had delivered at least two of these systems.

Advantages of Turnkey Systems

The advantages of procuring a turnkey system are:

• Low cost: From 50% to 80% of the costs of developing an automated system are usually incurred in systems design and programming; the balance of the cost is for hardware. The turnkey vendor is able to spread the software cost over a number of installations so that a single customer pays as little as 3% of the software development cost.

• Firm price: The contracted price of the turnkey system will be all that the library pays, even if the vendor incurs costs that were not anticipated when the contract was signed (unless, of course, the specifications are modified after the contract is negotiated).

• Firm delivery date: The installation dates for turnkey systems are generally 90 to 120 days from receipt of the order. However, any custom developments, for features not available from the vendor at the time the order is placed, often take a year or more.

• Known features: The features of a turnkey system are known when the contract is signed. The performance of the features can usually be determined by looking at the system installed in one or more comparable libraries.

• Dynamic system design: The competition among the turnkey vendors assures a library of continuous software enhancements. The general practice is to include all future improvements in the software maintenance contract, available at a monthly cost (typically $400). No programmers are, therefore, needed in the library.

Disadvantages of Turnkey Systems

Historically, the most significant disadvantage of turnkey systems has been that the library could not customize a system to its special needs. This concern is rapidly disappearing as turnkey systems have become parameterized, or table-driven (i.e., containing various options from which the user can choose). Another problem has been vendors that have withdrawn from the market. Libraries should take care to select a vendor that is financially viable and committed to the library automation market.

Evaluating Turnkey Systems

All of the major turnkey vendors are typically able to offer 90% or more of the features included in a library's specifications. They differ mainly in their choice of hardware and software and in their development schedules. For example, Geac in mid-1983 offered a powerful system with highly expandable hardware, but with a proprietary programming language that is hardware-dependent. While the fact that Geac manufactures its own CPUs substantially ameliorates danger of outgrowing the machine, a library runs the risk that the company might cease to market automated library systems.

In contrast, DataPhase was using transportable software that is relatively independent of the hardware choice. The hardware itself is quite expandable. However, in 1982 the company got so bogged down in the development of an even more powerful system configured around a super-mini of a different make that it fell behind in delivery of enhancements to systems already installed. As the result of this conflict in development priorities, Data-Phase's reputation suffered and sales declined dramatically. As of mid-1983, a major reorganization had taken place, and the company had focused its attention on serving existing customers rather than on making new sales. By fall 1983, it was still too early to assess the effectiveness of the new strategy. (The problems of DataPhase, including its dispute with the Chicago Public Library, will be discussed further later in this chapter.)

The evaluation of the vendors should therefore be much more broadly based than a comparison of functions. It should include the vendor's financial viability, past performance and ability to maintain its development program, and the position of the library should the vendor leave the marketplace.

SOFTWARE PACKAGES

Rather than purchasing hardware and software from a single source, one can purchase them separately. A library might choose this approach because it can obtain hardware at a discount or because it already has hardware available to it. The greatest risk with purchasing a software package, whether from another library or a commercial vendor, is that no one takes responsibility for the hardware and software working together. The library runs a real risk that the hardware vendor will claim that problems in system performance are attributable to the software and that the software supplier will say it is a hardware problem.

Software from Turnkey Vendors

Some turnkey vendors will sell their software separately. However, while the cost of an integrated multifunction software package is usually $30,000 to $60,000 when purchased as part of a turnkey system, the price is typically one-third to one-half higher when purchased without hardware. This is because the turnkey vendors make most of their profit from the sale of hardware. When the hardware sale is not realized, part of the lost profit is recovered by increasing the price for the software.

Software packages are available from Avatar for the Digital Equipment Corp. DEC PDP 11, Data General Eclipse and IBM Series 1 equipment; from CTI for Microdata or Prime equipment; and from Universal for DEC VAX equipment. The Universal software is less complete than the Avatar and CTI packages.

Other Software Packages

Most available software packages are not supported in the same sense in which software that is part of a turnkey system is supported. There is no committed development schedule for enhancements and additional modules, and less training may be offered as well. As

IBM states in its descriptions of DOBIS/Leuven: "It is a customer-installed and maintained product."

Additionally, the fact that one or more of the packages may be designed for the hardware that is available to a library does not guarantee that the package is usable. Most of the library packages were designed to operate on a dedicated machine. It is, therefore, important that a careful analysis be made to determine that the software package can be operated in combination with the other applications already on the machine. The developers of the packages have selected operating systems and data base management systems that are uniquely suited to the manipulation of bibliographic records. A particularly popular choice has been MIIS/MUMPS, which is a unique bundling of operating system, data base management system and programming language into one system development package. (See the description of MIIS/MUMPS in Chapter 3.)

Three major commercially available software packages in mid-1983 were NOTIS, DOBIS/Leuven and VTLS.

NOTIS

Northwestern University offers its NOTIS integrated multifunction software package for IBM 4300 series machines at a price of $50,000. The system includes acquisitions, processing, serials and circulation control modules.

Although NOTIS has been available for purchase since 1971, it has not been fully supported and has been burdened by its outdated circulation system, relying on punched cards rather than on bar code or OCR technology. In 1983 Northwestern University announced that it would commercially market the system, upgrade the circulation module and begin to provide ongoing support comparable to that available with turnkey systems. Representations were also made that Northwestern would assume responsibility for hardware-software compatibility. If NOTIS succeeds, it may influence other software vendors to provide turnkey-type support.

NOTIS is, however, only suitable for a large-library environment. Any library with fewer than 100 terminals would be ill-advised to implement a mainframe-based automation program.

DOBIS/Leuven

DOBIS/Leuven was developed by IBM for the Universities of Dortmund (Germany) and Leuven (Belgium). DOBIS is oriented to technical services and Leuven to public services. However, they are generally sold together, and in the United States the system is usually simply called DOBIS. The system supports cataloging, searching, acquisitions and circulation. In mid-1983, IBM announced the availability of serials control software, completing the technical services component of DOBIS. The system runs on IBM mainframe equipment (such as the IBM 370/138). The software is leased for a period of 24 months, after which the user has a paid-up license. Depending on which operating system is used, the approximate cost is either $36,000 or $50,000. Because DOBIS, like NOTIS, is a mainframe-based system, it is most suitable for large libraries.

VTLS

Virginia Polytechnic Institute, or Virginia Tech, offers its VTLS integrated software package for the Hewlett-Packard 3000 minicomputers, which are comparable to the mid-sized machines most often used by turnkey vendors. VTLS supports circulation, acquisitions and a public access catalog. It was designed specifically for an academic library, but several sales have been made to public libraries, and the software has been modified to accommodate public library needs. Revenues were still not sufficient, as of mid-1983, to pay for ongoing development costs, a common occurrence when a library seeks to sell its software package to other libraries. Nevertheless, prospects were good, because VTLS is the most successful software package in the history of library automation.

IN-HOUSE DEVELOPMENT

The great benefit of in-house development is substantial control over the design of the system; all the functions the library wants can be included. The library must, however, have electronic data processing expertise on the staff. It is particularly important that a library not rely on a single individual, since the project could bog down if that person were to leave.

The equipment for a minicomputer-based system can cost as little as $100,000, but the development of the software or instructions to operate the system can cost several times that much. In 1983 more than 80% of a typical locally developed system's cost was for software. Why? Because advances in technology have resulted in steadily declining hardware prices while software productivity has shown no comparable improvement. The Rand Corporation forecast this trend as early as 1972, when it reported that software costs, which represented 15% of total costs in 1955, had risen to 70% by 1970 and would go to 85% by the mid-1980s.

Outstanding examples of in-house development are the integrated or comprehensive systems of the University of Chicago, Northwestern University, Stanford University and the University of Toronto. The Stanford and Toronto systems have subsequently evolved into bibliographic utilities serving dozens of libraries under the names Research Libraries Information Network (RLIN) and University of Toronto Library Automated Systems (UTLAS). NOTIS, as mentioned above, is being offered to other libraries as a software package. All these systems were done with very large computers, requiring the commitment of millions of dollars and several years of development time.

While most institutions have not had the human or financial resources to develop integrated systems with acquisitions, cataloging, serials and circulation functions, more than 400 libraries have accomplished in-house automation of a single function. The most popular applications have been acquisitions, circulation and serials holdings lists. As turnkey systems have become more widely available, there has been less incentive for libraries to create their own systems.

Many of the in-house developments have been described in professional library journals. A search through *Library Literature* back to 1967 will identify more than 100 articles on the subject. The systems described in the literature are almost all configured around large mainframe computers. Today, however, libraries have the choice of undertaking development of a system on a less expensive minicomputer.

VENDOR-PROVIDED SERVICES

A library may avoid making a capital investment in computer hardware and software by contracting with a vendor to supply automation support services. The contract may be for an integrated system or for the support of a single function, usually acquisitions or serials. Such services have been available from several sources including turnkey vendors and book and serial jobbers.

Gaylord Bros., Inc. was the first vendor to enter this market. As early as 1978 it offered a distributed turnkey circulation system. The distributed system—which consists of a host computer at the vendor and a smaller computer at the library—attempts to offer libraries the lower initial capital cost of a distributed system, in which the host computer already exists, and the predictable operating costs and features of a standard turnkey package. The principal pricing formula used is one of charging by the transaction. It appears that the combined capital cost and operating costs over a five-year period would not favor this type of system. Not surprisingly, then, the customer base for the distributed system did not grow between 1980 and 1983. Nevertheless, several libraries have relied on this approach for three or more years. Recently Gaylord has been promoting this service less actively. Instead, it has been putting greater emphasis on its small turnkey systems based on personal microcomputers.

Avatar, one of the newer turnkey vendors, began offering a service bureau approach to automation in 1982. Libraries in the Mid-Atlantic area can lease one or more ports on equipment operated by Avatar and have access to data storage hardware and software for several functions. The capabilities of the service bureau system are the same as the stand-alone mini-based Avatar system, but no capital outlay is required. The typical cost of a single terminal in 1983 was about $600 per month. In mid-1983 there were three users of this system; all had only one terminal. That is understandable because the cost of using multiple terminals on a remote system over several years would add up to more than the cost of a stand-alone system.

Sigma Data Computing Corp. is a particular type of turnkey vendor, specializing in providing custom-tailored software with hardware. The company undertook the development and management of a shared acquisitions system for several federal libraries in 1981. Each institution could not only obtain access to a shared automated system, but also participate in the development of future modules. While there were no cost savings realized by this approach, it apparently fit the political and budgetary requirements of the agencies.

The most successful vendor-operated systems have been the acquisitions systems offered by the book and serial jobbers: LIBRIS II from Baker & Taylor Co., OLAS from Brodart,

Inc., LINCS from F.W. Faxon Co., Inc. and OSS from Ebsco Subscription Services. They all provide libraries not only hardware and software, but also access to the vendor's data base and electronic messaging system. In each case the vendor developed the service to promote its principal business of book or serials jobbing. Pricing is generally by the month and favors libraries that do a large volume of ordering. None of the vendors are making money on their automated services, but they believe that customers who use a vendor's automated system send a larger percentage of their orders to that vendor. There is also the expectation that order fulfillment costs will be reduced as more orders are received online. These vendors are constantly reexamining their services, however, because the primary motivation of most of these firms is selling library materials, rather than supplying automation support.

BIBLIOGRAPHIC UTILITY SYSTEMS

Reliance on a bibliographic utility—Online Computer Library Center, Inc. (OCLC), RLIN, UTLAS or Washington Library Network (WLN)—has been highly successful for cataloging. The extremely large data bases necessary for cataloging require a very large capital investment and a skilled staff of library automation specialists. The data base of a bibliographic utility may have several million bibliographic records. That large a file requires dozens of disk drives to store the information and several computers to manipulate it.

By mid-1983 the utilities were offering not only cataloging, but also acquisitions and interlibrary loan support. OCLC also offered serials control. All services were priced by the transaction. For smaller libraries this basis of charging is particularly beneficial. Some libraries pay as little as $4000 per year and have access to more than $40 million in computer equipment and a data base of 9 million titles. Large libraries may find the utility approach expensive for everything but cataloging support.

A library usually selects the utility on the basis of the size and type of data base rather than the type of equipment used. It is, therefore, not essential that a librarian have knowledge of the large computer systems used by the networks.

PARENT ORGANIZATION FACILITIES

Using the computer facilities and data processing personnel in a library's parent organization has the advantage of dramatically reducing the capital expenditure required for automation. The design of the system, however, must fit into broader institutional procedures and priorities. The system may therefore end up less than ideally suited to library applications.

As with the in-house development of a stand-alone system, software development will be time-consuming, and the costs are difficult to predict. Many libraries have found it useful to retain a software development firm that specializes in library software to do at least part of the work. This avoids an extensive period of education for the central computer center staff, who may be unfamiliar with the particular needs of libraries.

SHARING A SYSTEM

The limited capacity of all but mainframe computers until the late 1970s was responsible for most libraries choosing to acquire a stand-alone system that served only the one library. By 1978, however, a number of public libraries had begun to share automated circulation systems.

Public, Academic and Multitype Library Consortia

One of the most successful shared systems is that of the North Suburban Library System in metropolitan Chicago. As many as 22 libraries share a single computer, with some of the members paying as little as $600 per month for a single terminal, access to the shared bibliographic files, storage space for copy specific and patron information, and printing facilities for the printing of notices and reports. (See Chapter 7 for more information on system sharing in Illinois.) Several hundred public libraries in other states have installed similar shared systems.

Academic libraries have until recently not participated to a large extent in shared systems. This is partly because the existing consortia have emphasized circulation control, without provision for the addition of other functions at a later time, and also because of concerns about governance in systems dominated by public libraries.

Until recently, those academic library consortia that have been developed to sponsor library automation have used mainframe computers. The costs have been high and flexibility was limited because of the large number of participants needed to justify the investment. Several academic library groups have now set up consortia to procure and manage automated library systems configured around turnkey minicomputer systems. Among the largest of these is the Pioneer Valley Cooperative of Massachusetts, which will tie together five institutions with combined resources of more than 3.7 million volumes. (The institutions are the University of Massachusetts, Amherst College, Mt. Holyoke College, Hampshire College and Smith College.)

Multitype library consortia are still rare. The Capitol Region (CT) and Southwestern Connecticut Regional Systems include several academic and public libraries. Because most library automation software is table-driven, each library can meet its individual needs with regard to specific operational functions and screen and report formats. The major issue in the case of multitype systems has not been system design, but governance: bringing libraries with only limited cooperative experience together in a joint program.

Economic Considerations

The primary economic consideration in the sharing of a system is geographic: it is rarely cost-effective for libraries more than 30 miles from each other to share a system, because ongoing telecommunications costs rapidly offset and exceed the capital cost of duplicating minicomputer hardware at separate locations. In most cases, the libraries should be within 12 miles of the central site. The rates for dedicated lines within a state are usually from $7 to $14 per mile per month. If an installation had 10 terminals, the cost of such a permanent connection to a central processing unit (CPU) 30 miles away would be $2400 per month, assuming an average charge over five years of $8 per mile per month. For the five-year period, that would be $144,000, which would almost pay for the duplication of the central site hardware and software. (Rates may also increase dramatically in the aftermath of the AT&T divestiture of local telephone service.) While it is possible to reduce ongoing telecommunications costs by having terminals share a line, one then increases the capital and maintenance costs for multiplexors and other telecommunications hardware.

Thus, there are only limited economic benefits in sharing a computer system, even for libraries relatively close together. However, there can be significant service benefits. If the libraries have complementary collections and already have a history of interlibrary lending and reciprocal borrowing, the sharing of the data base can facilitate and strengthen these services. Public libraries that have shared computer systems report a doubling of interlibrary loan within the first 12 months. Patrons also appear to be more likely to visit other libraries in the system besides their "home" library. These changes can themselves lead to higher costs (e.g., for item delivery and personnel). Therefore, libraries should consider sharing systems only if they are prepared for substantial increases in the flow of materials and patrons among them.

Benefits of Resource Sharing

The greatest benefit of shared systems, then, is not cost reductions in the performance of library functions in each library, but the creation of a common online holdings file that facilitates resource sharing. At the most immediate level, the existence of such a shared holdings file could be expected to streamline and increase interlibrary lending. The file would speed up the identification of which of the cooperating libraries holds a wanted item and provide information as to whether it is currently available for loan. The electronic transmission of the loan request would speed processing of the loan, and the ability to electronically record "holds" against an item would improve turnaround time for checking in loaned material and matching a returned item to a waiting request. Automatic monitoring of loan and hold requests would provide library staff with immediate warnings when demand for an item exceeds a predetermined level, permitting the prompt placement of orders for extra copies or alteration of the loan period for items subject to heavy demand.

In the longer term, the availability of these and other statistics on collection use would allow the libraries to more finely tune their collection development policies. Access to online holdings, selection lists and acquisition files would enable libraries in the group to make purchasing decisions that mesh with reliable information about the holdings or outstanding orders of other members of the cooperative. The use of shared systems can facilitate the shared funding of expensive items or "only one copy needed in the group" purchases. All of these would be voluntary actions taken in response to the known actions of other libraries.

A year or more of successful sharing of a computer system would be necessary before there would be sufficient confidence in the technology to launch this type of cooperation. If a group of libraries were able to cooperate successfully for three to five years, it might be possible to coordinate the actual development of collections, assigning roles to the participating institutions and relocating holdings among the libraries as deemed desirable. The ability of the computer system(s) to easily record and keep track of changes in the location of library materials would make it possible to implement such a program.

Problems of Resource Sharing

These and other resource sharing applications would considerably enhance each library's capacity to meet and respond to changes in its users' requirements. However, while it is relatively simple to improve the mechanics of interlibrary lending, it is extremely difficult to coordinate collection development. Librarians are understandably reluctant to reduce their collections on the basis of another library's commitment to acquire in that area and to be responsive to requests for use of the materials. What happens if the resource library has to reduce its collecting effort or if a change in adminstration results in less commitment to meeting the needs of other libraries? Librarians in large libraries may worry that the demand placed upon them will exceed the benefits of resource sharing. The concept of resource sharing is particularly difficult to sell to faculty on academic campuses who may fear that resource sharing programs are merely devices for reducing acquisitions budgets.

Other Considerations

As difficult as resource sharing is, it is the primary justification for installing a shared automated system. If the real motive for considering a shared system is the automation of internal library functions, it would be more cost-effective to procure stand-alone systems and arrange for dial-up access to the systems of a limited number of libraries that have complementary holdings. The terminals of any one system can then be used to search the data bases of the other systems to determine holdings and availability and to request an interlibrary loan. The major limitation is the ability of staff to become and remain familiar with the searching and messaging requirements of more than two or three systems.

This does not mean that the only way to launch a shared system is to sign a formal contract spelling out that the group is committed to cooperative collection development. It might be enough that the participants commit themselves to increasing interlibrary loan as a percentage of total circulation from the typical relatively low level of 1% to 3% of circulation activity to a level of at least 5% to 7% of circulation activity. At that increased level of activity, the additional telecommunications costs associated with shared systems would be justified.

There are important governance issues to be addressed when libraries share a system. A decision must first be made whether the libraries are equal partners or whether one institution owns the system and sells services to the others. It they are equal partners, committees will have to be established to determine such matters as what bibliographic standards shall prevail, what rates shall be charged to the participants and how decisions about expansion of system capabilities shall be reached. The decision-making process is likely to be time-consuming—often two or more years to select, procure and implement a system when six or more institutions are involved. The length and complexity of the process has prompted some academic libraries to plan systems for themselves, but with capacities large enough to bring in other libraries at a later date. While this is technologically feasible, it may be politically unwise to plan without involving potential participants.

SINGLE- AND MULTIFUNCTION SYSTEMS

Almost all of the automated library systems that were undertaken in the 1970s were single-function systems, primarily turnkey systems for circulation control. In addition, more than 300 libraries developed their own software, usually for acqusitions or circulation control; most of these developments occurred in the 1960s and early 1970s.

Until recently, only a few dozen libraries had sought to develop systems that included several functions. Librarians have not proceeded out of ignorance. The literature of librarianship has been discussing the "total systems approach" since the early 1960s. At that time, however, the cost of available mainframe computers was too high for most libraries to afford. The majority of the academic libraries that automated had to make use of the campus computer center's facilities and staff. They often had to compete against teaching and research programs for scarce machine and human resources. It is not surprising that most libraries automated only a single function.

The advent of minicomputers in the 1970s gave libraries the opportunity to automate without competing for the resources of a parent organization's computer center. Unfortunately, the limited capacities of the early minicomputers, usually less than 128,000 characters (128KB) of primary memory, still restricted most libraries to the automation of a single function.

The high cost of custom development brought commercial firms into the picture. In 1973 CLSI began to market a minicomputer-based system for acquisitions control. While nine systems were actually installed, the concept was a failure because the acquisitions practices of libraries varied too much to make it possible for them to use the simple standard software package that was offered. CLSI subsequently tried circulation control and found that the circulation procedures of libraries are much more similar than the acquisitions procedures. The initial installation made at the Marin County (CA) Public Library in 1974 is still functioning today, although the system software has been enhanced many times. Nearly 250 other CLSI circulation systems have been installed since 1974.

Recently the capacities and operating speeds of minicomputers have increased to exceed those of the mainframe computers of the 1960s, but at a fraction of the cost. The typical minicomputer used for library automation in 1983 can be expanded to 2 million characters of primary memory, or 16 times that of the machines of 1975. Super-minis can be expanded to more than 6 million characters of primary memory. There is now no technical restriction on placing several functions on a minicomputer. Theoretically one could key in the book order as part of the acquisitions subsystem; catalog the book when received, creating an online or patron access catalog; and control the circulation of the item beginning with the patron's presentation of it at a circulation terminal. An interlibrary loan subsystem could link the library's system to that of other libraries.

What is lacking, however, is a comprehensive bibliographic data base against which to match the original title selection. The determination and keying of the entire bibliographic record from scratch is expensive. It is, therefore, necessary to continue to rely on a bibliographic utility as a source for current cataloging records. The utility is the data bank from which the library draws to build the local data base. Once the record is in the local data base, it is possible to use it for the writing of a purchase order, the creation of an online catalog or the attachment of circulation control records.

PROTECTION AGAINST OUTGROWING THE SYSTEM

The potential automation of several functions using a single computer and/or the sharing of the computer with one or more other libraries raise the prospect of outgrowing the computer system and incurring high costs to procure another system. Libraries can protect themselves against this possibility by looking to the expandability of the hardware and the transportability or transferability of the software.

Hardware Expandability

The central processing unit of a system installed by a medium-sized library should have a primary memory that can be expanded to at least 1 MB or 1 million characters; a system CPU for a large library should be expandable to at least 2 MB. A consortium that includes a large library should have even greater expansion capability. Ideally, vendors should also offer the option of multiprocessing, so that additional machines can be linked with the original machine if necessary.

The error that libraries have most often made in automating with minicomputers has been to purchase systems with CPUs that are too small to accommodate expansion if library circulation increases, neighboring libraries are added to the system, and/or other functions are added. Because CPUs installed in minicomputer-based circulation systems before 1979 had only 128 KB (128,000 characters) or less of primary memory, more than a score of libraries have had to "swap out," or exchange, their small CPUs for larger ones at a cost of $10,000 to $50,000. In contrast, if a library requires at the outset that the CPU provided have the capability of expansion to 1 or 2 MB, the extra one-time cost of that capability should not exceed $6000, and the addition of the actual memory later on will cost the same as would increasing the memory of a smaller CPU up to its capacity—not more than $5000 per 128 KB.

Multiprocessing, or the wiring of two or more adjacent CPUs together to increase processing capacity without disposing of the old machine, is well within the state of the art, although only CLSI and Data Research Associates had installed a multi-CPU system in a library as of mid-1983. Wiring machines together is not always efficient, however. CLSI had intended to use DECNET, its computer manufacturer's networking software, but it discovered that its use would require a considerable amount of the computing resources of the CPUs, resulting in an adverse impact on the response time of the system. CLSI, therefore, undertook to develop its own linkage among its CPUs. It required more than two years to create the prototype system using the PDP 11/34 and several months more to tie PDP 11/44s together. Recently CLSI has also successfully linked machines of different sizes, such as the powerful 11/44 with the small but efficient 11/23.

Transportability of Software

Other turnkey system vendors have, for the most part, sought to transport their software to larger computers to avoid the linking of computers. The initial choice of programming language and dramatic increases in the sizes of computers have made this possible for CTI, which offers its software on Datamedia micros, Microdata minis and Prime superminis.

However, some automated library systems employ programming languages that are hardware-dependent; that is, they can only operate on one line of machines. This is the case with CLSI. The applications software was written to realize maximum efficiency from particular computer equipment. That was deemed important when minicomputers were limited in their capacities. Today, as discussed above, the capabilities and cost of hardware are of less concern than the labor cost of developing and maintaining software.

The ability to rewrite the software with the expenditure of only a moderate amount of money and time, so that it will run on a much larger computer or a different one, is highly desirable. If the vendor does not offer highly transportable software, it must offer another alternative to the library, because no one knows exactly what the full impact of adding new modules will be, particularly patron access catalogs with Boolean searching capability (i.e., the capability to link terms in a search by AND, OR, NOT). A library that may later decide to implement a patron access catalog must recognize that a change of hardware may be required because of unanticipated demands of the patron access catalog function on the computer hardware.

INTERFACES

As mentioned in the section on single- and multifunction systems, currently available systems rely on the bibliographic data base of a bibliographic utility to achieve low-cost cataloging. In-house systems must therefore have an interface, or electronic linkage, to the bibliographic utility's system. It is also possible that a library may choose the system of a turnkey vendor for circulation and the online catalog but would prefer to use the acquisitions system of a book jobber because it offers online ordering capability. Ideally, an interface would exist between the in-house system and that of the jobber. The ability to communicate with the systems of other nearby libraries again would involve interfaces.

Connecting Distant or Foreign Systems

Telecommunications and special networking software, rather than direct wiring, are required to link identical systems that are at some distance from one another. That is within the state of the art. However, computer-to-computer interfaces involving distant systems with identical hardware and software have not yet been established in a library environment. Further, a large library or group of libraries that automates today must not only deal with the question of linking the CPUs in a single system or connecting two identical distant systems, but also with the possible linking of a system with a "foreign" system. That has been successfully done between the terminal of a turnkey system and OCLC, as well as between a turnkey system terminal and the CPU of another system, but not directly between CPUs.

The movement of bibliographic data among these dissimilar systems poses technical, economic and political obstacles that require some analysis. Most of the initial research and application in the area of computer-to-computer interfaces appears to have been motivated by the desire to fully use expensive computer resources rather than to facilitate the movement of large amounts of information. Most of the oldest computer networks link large mainframe computers in several large computing centers. More recent work has focused on distributed processing, the creation of multiprocessor systems for large companies and government agencies that wish to decentralize their computer systems while retaining central control.

In distributed processing, a large number of minicomputers have typically been dispersed geographically, and all have been linked with a host computer at a central site. With few exceptions, these distributed systems have had a highly centralized structure with most of the processing power concentrated in one large central installation. This has been the case because highly centralized systems have been easier to design, operate and control than decentralized systems. Even though a distributed system might involve more than one hardware type, they have been centrally planned systems in which software could be developed for the total system by or for the system's owner. In other words, multijurisdictional problems have been avoided.

The Unique Requirements of Libraries

In the case of two or more libraries with turnkey systems from different vendors, several independently and fully developed systems would need to be linked. Such an effort involves connecting computer systems with different hardware and different software using various programming languages, some of them proprietary and confidential. There may also be different file structures, operational features, command languages, record access methods, indexing methods, system performance priorities and so forth.

Most important of all, the competing vendors may have little incentive to cooperate with one another. The vendor that is the most firmly established in a locality benefits from the inability of other systems to link with its system. This creates a problem for a library planning to purchase a turnkey system and needing to link its system with one or more existing local systems. The library may be pressured to match the system(s) already installed and so not select the system that best meets its unique needs.

Computer-to-computer interfaces are particularly difficult to achieve, but direct communication between or among different systems has the advantage of providing full access to and full control of all files, except as restrictions may be imposed for administrative reasons. For example, a library could update the patron records on any of the computers to reflect a delinquency. And, in addition to searching the holdings of another library, a library could place a hold or perform an interlibrary loan charge-out transaction.

STANDARDS FOR COMPUTER-TO-COMPUTER COMMUNICATION

Requirements for computer-to-computer communication among "foreign" or dissimilar systems requires the adoption of protocols, or standards, for linking systems. There are at present no protocols for the electronic communication of digital information among libraries in a network. A number of protocols developed for other applications do exist. These might be used in the development of protocols for libraries, but a great deal of additional work would have to be done.

There is a proposed protocol for libraries developed by a task force appointed by the National Commission on Libraries and Information Science and the National Bureau of Standards. The formulation of this protocol represents the completion of one major, time-consuming technical task in the laying of the groundwork for a multisystem library network, but much remains to be done. The task force envisioned only the linking of bibliographic utilities, the Library of Congress and other major nodes in a national cataloging and reference service network. The task force specifically recommended that acquisitions and circulation control be handled locally by turnkey systems and made no provision for connecting these systems with one another or with any emerging national network.

Thus, the major U.S. effort to develop protocols for libraries is of little help to libraries attempting to connect turnkey systems. Too little work has been done, and the recommendations focus national efforts chiefly on the linking of shared cataloging systems.

THE ATTITUDES OF TURNKEY VENDORS

As a consultant, the author has on several occasions interviewed a number of turnkey vendors. While none refused to consider the development of a computer-to-computer interface with systems supplied by other vendors, all qualified their responses. One firm insisted that the cost would be prohibitive because more than 100 man-years of time would be required to develop the software. Three other estimates fell in the range of 4 to 20 man-years. One vendor stated that it could not enter into a contract to participate in such a development unless a vendor performance measurement tool were developed, so it could be paid when it had performed its share of the specified work. This position was taken to protect it against the possibility of nonpayment because of failure or unwillingness to perform on the part of another vendor. A library or library consortium that agreed to this approach might then incur substantial expense without achieving a working interface.

Thus, while computer-to-computer interfaces between foreign systems are within the state of the art, it appears that it will be several years before the obstacles will be overcome for turnkey library systems.

TERMINAL-TO-COMPUTER INTERFACES

There has been successful linkage among automated library systems through terminal-to-computer interfaces. This involves the use of a terminal of one automated system to access the computer of another automated system. The one-time software development cost of each such interface is estimated to be between $60,000 and $90,000. Several vendors have expressed a willingness to develop the necessary interfaces, although some have said such development would have to be a lower priority than linking the vendor's own systems.

CLSI, for example, is most concerned with linking CPUs that are standing next to one another. As of mid-1983, DataPhase appeared to have made the greatest progress in providing software support for libraries seeking to search other systems.

Many library administrators and staff members who have been interviewed by the author have expressed a preference for searching and message capability only. They prefer that libraries not be able to manipulate one another's systems and files. The terminal-to-computer interface would, therefore, meet this requirement, and it would not be necessary to fund expensive computer-to-computer interface development.

Searching several computer systems that have been linked using a terminal-to-computer interface can be frustrating. An operator at a terminal must dial up one system after the other, log on and conduct separate searches in order to locate one specific item. In addition, there are enough idiosyncracies in each separately developed data base that the operator must become and remain familiar with each one.

FRONT-END PROCESSORS AS EMULATORS

The libraries of the greater Denver-Boulder area in Colorado—known as the Irving Group—were pursuing yet another approach in mid-1983. The group had commissioned a consulting study on the general design and implementation of a data communications network connecting the computer systems in the five libraries. The libraries have both CLSI and DataPhase automated circulation systems.

The consultants recommended a system involving the placement of a front-end processor between each circulation system CPU and the telephone line. The interface will be programmed to emulate a computer terminal; the foreign automated circulation system will "see" the interface as one of its internal library terminals. In this way, the requirement for modifications by either turnkey vendor, CLSI or DataPhase, will be avoided. The transmission medium among libraries will be conventional voice-grade telephone lines. Other libraries may be able to participate in the network by dial-up access. The cost of the program over five years will be in excess of $450,000 because hardware must be purchased, programs written and telecommunications costs paid.

If the venture is successful, an interface may become available that would make it possible for a terminal operator to sequentially dial up several other systems without being expert in the unique protocols and characteristics of each. It is hoped that the cost of this capability would drop dramatically after the initial installation in Colorado.

PROFILES OF MAJOR TURNKEY VENDORS

A majority of libraries seeking to automate more than a single function will probably choose to purchase a turnkey system. The six established turnkey vendors are described briefly in this section. (Addresses and telephone numbers are listed in Appendix A.) All of the companies discussed have relatively mature multifunction systems that support the MARC format. All have installed at least six systems so that their performance can be evaluated. With the exception of Avatar, each has sold an average of at least $2.5 million in systems over the past two years.

AVATAR SYSTEMS, INC.

Avatar is the newest and smallest of the major turnkey vendors. It was started in 1981 by three librarians and systems analysts who left the National Library of Medicine, and it is dedicated to supporting the Integrated Library System (ILS) developed by NLM's Lister Hill Center for Biomedical Communications. Avatar plans to provide turnkey installations on Data General Eclipse, Digital Equipment Corporation PDP 11 and IBM Series/1 mini-computers. Some of the hardware options can be configured with up to 2 MB (2 megabytes or 2 million characters) of primary memory. Secondary storage up to 2400 MB is available. The wide range of hardware on which the software will run means that it is easy to tailor the system to the specific needs of a library or consortium.

Avatar has recently introduced a micro-based system configured around the DEC PDP 11/23. It is intended for libraries with fewer than 30,000 volumes. There is currently no super-mini option available for large libraries and consortia, nor has Avatar demonstrated a successful multiprocessor system. Expansion is, therefore, only possible by adding memory within a CPU or by exchanging a smaller unit for a larger one within the small to mid-sized minicomputer range.

ILS provides support for acquisitions, serials checkin, circulation control, patron access catalog and management information functions. While all these functions are now present in the software—which is not the case with the other turnkey systems—some of the functions are not yet fully developed. The least fully developed is serials control; the company predicts that this function will be completed by early 1984.

The incomplete nature of the ILS software results from Avatar's purchase of the conceptual software package developed by the Lister Hill Center, which deliberately left the software incomplete to permit purchasers to modify it for their particular requirements. While additional development of ILS was sponsored by Lister Hill as late as early 1983, by mid-1983 most development activity was being undertaken by Avatar for its turnkey products.

The software is written in MIIS/MUMPS, a variation of an ANSI standard language, which was discussed in Chapter 3. (The use of ANSI standard languages guarantees that there will be a supply of trained programmers that could work on the system and imposes certain industry-wide accepted standards.) MIIS/MUMPS is particularly well suited to the control of bibliographic records and lends itself to rapid programming.

Avatar has had substantial financial support from a venture capital syndicate and would appear to have the resources to complete the software development scheduled for 1983. The long-term viability of the company will depend on 1983 and 1984 sales. In 1982 the company achieved sales of less than $500,000. Sales will need to go to at least $2.5 million a year by 1984 for the company to succeed. The rate of sales in mid-1983 suggests that the firm has a good chance of achieving that level.

The basic software package is excellent, and the company's founders are competent librarians and systems analysts. How well they will market the product and manage the company remains to be seen. New companies often fail or dramatically change direction during their first three years. As of mid-1983, ten contracts had been signed. The largest system installed to date is a multibranch system at Carnegie-Mellon University. It is difficult to estimate what the cost of an Avatar system might be because the company has bid on only a few RFPs (requests for proposals).

In 1983 OCLC announced its intention to acquire Avatar. Should that occur, the financial viability of this system would be assured. Pricing practices and development schedules might be changed.

CL SYSTEMS, INC.

CL Systems, Inc. (CLSI) is the oldest of the turnkey library system vendors, having installed its first system in 1973. It also had the largest sales in the industry in 1982 ($15 million) and possibly the highest profit ($1 million). Over half of CLSI's sales were to existing clients who were expanding or upgrading their systems. DataPhase and Geac have actually had higher sales of new systems in the past two years, although the former has recently experienced a sharp downturn in sales.

The early entry of CLSI into the field has affected its development. CLSI has done much of its programming in assembly language, which is machine-dependent. (The system runs on DEC machines.) As previously mentioned, this was done to exploit the limited capacity of the minicomputers available in the early 1970s. Thus, CLSI was for some time limited by its software to the very small DEC PDP 11/04 and 11/05. The company has had to spend a considerable amount of money on software rewriting in order to offer the larger systems that libraries have begun to demand since the late 1970s. In 1978 it rewrote its software for the PDP 11/34, a mid-sized mini. It has recently rewritten the software again so that it can run on any of the PDP 11 line, including the relatively new and powerful PDP 11/44. Despite the inherent limitations of machine dependency, DEC Assembly is widely known and used. There would be little difficulty moving to any other PDP 11 series machine and there would be no difficulty in finding programmers were CLSI ever to stop supporting the system.

CLSI has begun to install systems that link several PDP 11/44s together into a multiprocessor system to accommodate very large libraries and library consortia. While this provides a good growth path, the cost of the larger systems tends to be high because of the need to link mid-sized minicomputers together instead of using a single super-mini.

Until recently, larger libraries have often been unhappy with the performance of the CLSI system, but smaller ones have been well satisfied. Large libraries have regularly complained about poor response time, high downtime and poor maintenance. These problems appeared to be diminishing in 1982 and 1983 as CLSI customers upgraded their systems to the multiprocessor configuration and as the company improved its maintenance program. Nevertheless, care must be taken in planning expansion of a CLSI system and particular attention must be paid to the maintenance contract.

CLSI has completed circulation control and patron access catalog software. Acquisitions and media booking software are in the final stages of development. There is no announced date for serials control, but company representatives estimate an early 1985 completion.

The cost of a CLSI system depends somewhat on how the RFP is written. CLSI's software is usually priced separately for each module. List prices are $20,000 to $50,000 per module. If the RFP requires that software be bid as a single integrated package—often described as "bundling" the software—the price is sometimes as low as $60,000 for all modules. The average CLSI system installed in 1983 sells for over $200,000, but mini-computer-based systems are available for as little as $140,000.

CTI LIBRARY SYSTEMS, INC.

CTI Library Systems, Inc. is a relatively new company. It was founded by Brigham Young University of Utah to market a microcomputer-based backup system that the University developed for its library's CLSI circulation control system. In the first year, 1980, more than 75 of the backup systems were sold to CLSI system users. The money was then invested in the development of other library systems. Increased financial resources became available when CTI was sold first to a Salt Lake City firm and later to Government Services Group of Sacramento, CA. Sales in 1982 were approximately $5 million, well above the minimum level required for viability.

In mid-1983 Government Services experienced considerable financial problems, and there was a prospect that the company would go bankrupt. The management of CTI sought to maintain its company at arms length from the parent, but as of September 1983, Government Services had reorganized and taken over day-to-day management of CTI. Several key CTI people left on short notice. It is therefore important that the company's present financial and managerial viability be investigated closely by a library considering procurement of its system.

The CTI system is designed around the PICK operating system, an operating system supported on six different hardware lines, including the Microdata minis, Prime super-minis and Datamedia micros. Microdata Corp. computers are manufactured by a subsidiary of McDonnell Douglas. The largest computer has a capacity of up to 2 MB, making it comparable to the DEC PDP 11/44 and Data General S/140 used by several other vendors. Government Services is a Prime dealer and has tended to promote that equipment rather than the Microdata line. Care should therefore be taken in arranging for hardware maintenance of Microdata equipment.

A unique feature of the Microdata and Prime computer lines is the REALITY data base management system, which is extremely well-suited for the control of data files. When used with the BASIC programming language, it offers considerable flexibility for designing library systems. It also permits a great deal of local modification without affecting the generic CTI software. However, one must be careful that the system does not become overburdened with additional software that has not been carefully planned.

All functions have been developed except serials control. No date has been set for its completion even though representations have been made to customers that it is on the development schedule. The media booking system is the most sophisticated of any available today.

A minimum system based on a Datamedia micro can be purchased for less than $50,000, but the product has not sold as well as the more powerful—and more expensive—PDP 11-based systems offered by Avatar and CLSI. Microdata-based systems are comparable in cost to CLSI and DataPhase systems, while the Prime-based systems were in 1983 the lowest priced super-mini systems available.

DATAPHASE SYSTEMS, INC.

DataPhase is part of a holding company that includes a major Midwest lithographic business and two computer systems houses. In the past two years DataPhase has sold more turnkey systems than any other vendor. Nearly 50 of the 70 units sold since 1977 have been sold since 1981. Annual revenues are believed to be in excess of $7.5 million.

In 1983 there were some complaints about the company's slowness in bringing up new installations. The company appears to be financially solvent, although it may be overcommitted in terms of new installations. Of particular concern is the delay in completing the Chicago Public Library system, the largest ever undertaken by a turnkey vendor. Were a breach of contract suit initiated, it might seriously affect the company's financial position. Concerns about the ability of the company to resolve the Chicago Public issue have apparently affected sales.

DataPhase's basic system, configured around a Data General S/140 Eclipse central processing unit, is competitive in capabilities and in hardware price with the PDP 11/44 configured system offered by CLSI and can be expanded to 2 MB of primary memory. The DG Eclipse computer line can be upgraded further to the Eclipse 250 or to an MV 6000, a DG super-mini.

DataPhase also offers a more powerful system configured around the Tandem Computers, Inc. Non-stop computer, the most powerful mini available, with primary memories of 32 MB when a multiprocessor system is used. This is the machine used by Chicago Public and by OCLC as the front- and back-ends of its extensive computer system. The software for the Tandem is written in COBOL. For libraries that already have a DataPhase system running on a Data General minicomputer, a changeover to the Tandem-based system would be time-consuming and might involve a period of parallel operation. The file structures and commands of the two systems are identical so terminal users would not be aware of a change in systems except as performance might be temporarily affected during a changeover. No library has yet made the changeover, so the costs and the amount of disruption to library services that would occur cannot be predicted.

The DataPhase programs are written in MIIS/MUMPS, which is transportable to other machines such as the DEC PDP 11 line. Acquisitions and circulation control are completed, and patron access catalog software has been installed in test sites. Media booking is under development and should be completed in early 1984. Commitments with regard to serials control have been very general; an early 1985 date is most likely.

All of the other vendors discussed in this chapter offer a micro as a backup device for circulation checkout and checkin when the central computer site is not operational. Data-Phase has lagged in providing this capability.

DataPhase systems are priced close to those of CLSI. The only difference is usually that DataPhase has, since its founding, adhered to the concept of bundling software at a fixed price of $50,000 as against most other vendors' practice of pricing modules separately.

GEAC CANADA LTD.

Geac is a Canadian firm specializing in turnkey online banking systems. It has also been highly successful with the design and manufacture of its own minicomputers, the GEAC 6000 and 8000. It is, therefore, a financially strong company. In 1983 total sales were in excess of $40 million and library system sales were at least $11 million.

Geac routinely installs systems with hundreds of terminals and very high transaction volumes. Its initial installation at Guelph University was one of the first to include circulation, acquisitions and online inquiry by the general public (by author, title and call number only as of fall 1983).

The GEAC 8000 uses a multimicroprocessor design so that one processor is committed to terminal control, a second to problem processing and a third to the disks. Yet another processor is available to support any of the functions. There is a Dual 8000 available for users who exceed the capacity of the 8000. The 6000 is a recently introduced multiprocessor system with more limited capacity than the 8000. All three of these are super-minis and would be suitable only for larger, more complex systems.

Geac uses a proprietary operating system and programming language for its applications software development. It is not transportable to other hardware. One must, therefore, rely on Geac to develop and maintain hardware large enough to meet a library's growing needs.

The terminals are also unique. It is not possible to put inexpensive ASCII-type terminals on the system except in dial-up mode. All of the other systems discussed here allow libraries to use inexpensive terminals of their own choosing and obtain full access to all files.

Geac has been installed not only at the Guelph University Library, but also at the University of Waterloo (Ontario), the University of Arizona, New York University, the University of Southern California and Yale University. Geac is serving several consortia of libraries. More than 44 systems have been sold to date.

Acquisitions and circulation control software are fully developed. Media booking is almost completed. Serials control will be part of an enhanced acquisitions package scheduled for 1984. Patron access catalog software is currently installed at a test site at the New York University Library.

Geac was selected by OCLC as the most desirable "front-end" for its distributed processing system. (All of the turnkey systems now on the market were considered except Avatar, which had not then been launched, and DataPhase, which declined to participate in the OCLC investigation.) Although negotiations between OCLC and Geac were not successful, the selection of Geac on the basis of a critical comparative study is noteworthy. Unfortunately the confidential report is not available.

Because Geac uses super-minis, a typical medium-sized installation will be 15% or more above the price quoted by CLSI, DataPhase or other vendors. Geac is, however, extremely price-competitive when a large system is sought.

UNIVERSAL LIBRARY SYSTEMS, LTD.

The ULISYS system was originally developed in a Canadian academic institution and was subsequently purchased by J.A. Speight and Associates, a software firm with offices in Vancouver and Toronto. A new company, Universal Library Systems, was formed in 1976 to market the software as part of a turnkey online system. The first system was sold to the Phoenix Public Library in 1977. By 1982 annual sales were in excess of $2.5 million a year (author's estimate). As of late 1983 Universal had sold 20 systems, of which two-thirds had been installed and accepted.

ULISYS has used a variety of DEC machines, but most of its systems are configured around the PDP 11/70 or the VAX 11/730 through 780. Recently it has only bid the VAX series. The 11/780 is a super-mini that can support more than 100 terminals, a maximum primary memory of 12 MB and disk storage of up to 4096 MB. The availability of the powerful 11/780 provides libraries the opportunity to upgrade their systems to meet increased loads. The use of such powerful hardware usually means ULISYS systems are more expensive than CLSI or DataPhase.

The system is programmed in BASIC Plus, a language that does not accord with ANSI standards. Transfer of the software to another line of hardware would therefore be difficult. Universal describes ULISYS as including a data base management system and views the system architecture and file organization techniques as including unique and original proprietary features. Universal is one of the few turnkey vendors that has been prepared to sell its software alone at the same price as when it is part of a turnkey package.

Despite Universal's small size, libraries with ULISYS seem to be generally pleased with the company's level of support and commitment to service. A public library noted problems with unrealistic time projections for hardware delivery and software enhancements, and an academic library expressed a minor complaint about delays in software support but also indicated that the company was "extremely responsive to our needs."

Universal has installed one shared system for a group of libraries that want to share a data base, but require different call number formats, loan periods, etc.

As with most turnkey systems, ULISYS offers a mature circulation control system. It also provides an online authority file against which new records are validated before they are entered into the data base, and an online OCLC interface is operational. The company has indicated that it will soon implement similar interfaces with WLN and UTLAS. Universal also offers assistance in the conversion process by providing software that allows one library's data base to serve as the basis for building another library's data base.

Subject searching was first offered in 1977. The system now provides a public access catalog as well. A message function allows sending messages within a single library's system or, through a dial-access terminal, to another ULISYS system. An information and referral system permits the creation of community information files. Modules in development include acquisitions, film booking and serials control.

The ULISYS software is priced at up to $47,500, depending on the hardware configuration selected. Software maintenance charges are generally lower than those of the other vendors because Universal does not guarantee that features developed subsequent to an installation will be loaded retrospectively. Thus, unlike most turnkey systems, Universal systems do not all have identical software. By 1981 the ULISYS system as installed in Phoenix was totally out of date, lacking the sophistication and flexibility of later versions. The older software was replaced with the latest version and the existing data base converted to the radically different format required by the new software. No hardware changes were necessary. The company intends to establish one standard complete version of ULISYS.

OTHER TURNKEY VENDORS

Appendix A of this book also lists five other turnkey vendors that libraries might wish to consider.

As of mid-1983 Data Research Associates, Inc. was still in the middle of an ambitious installation program. If several systems are accepted by mid-1984, the company could establish a niche for itself as a supplier of large systems.

The future of Systems Control, Inc. in the marketplace is uncertain; as of mid-1983, it continued to experience significant difficulties in achieving satisfactory performance with the system it installed at the Montgomery County (MD) public libraries.

Gaylord's sales of mini-based systems and distributed circulation services appeared to be on a plateau in 1983. All existing systems supported only circulation control, and there is no evidence that other functions are in development. The company was embarked on a vigorous program of marketing software, hardware and supplies for small micro-based systems, but none had multifunction capability.

Sigma Data systems are unique in that they are highly customized. They have been most popular with federal and corporate libraries that are required to do a great deal of special reporting and financial control not common for libraries generally served by the turnkey market.

Easy Data Systems, Ltd. has achieved some success in 1983 in supplying small systems to special libraries, primarily in large corporations. There is no evidence that the company plans to enter the general library automation market.

SUMMARY

Libraries investigating automated systems have many alternatives from which to choose. Most popular is selection of a turnkey system, in which the vendor supplies hardware, software, installation, training and ongoing support. Other options are purchasing a software package for use on already available equipment, developing an in-house system, contracting for a commercial service, contracting with a bibliographic utility and relying on the facilities of a parent organization. The possibilities of system sharing should also be explored. There is a clear trend toward the use of integrated multifunction systems.

A major unresolved issue is the connection of distant and/or "foreign" systems. Although some success has been achieved in linking CPUs and terminals, computer-to-computer interfaces among library systems do not yet exist. Such interfaces would be highly advantageous, but they require communications protocols, which are both difficult and expensive to develop. It is unlikely that they will exist among turnkey systems in the near future.

Whichever automation option the library pursues, it must go through a careful planning and implementation process. Chapter 7 offers guidelines to help the library manager in the process.

7

Planning and Implementation

A library automation program should involve more complex, time-consuming and costly planning processes than other library programs because the impact of automation is so pervasive. In addition to significant budgetary implications, automation can require organizational changes, revisions in library policies and procedures, changes in the attitudes of both staff and patrons, and complex contractual obligations. Automation is too complex and costly to undertake without first engaging in extensive investigation, discussion and decision making.

RISKS IN AUTOMATING

Automation also involves taking chances, even if the library has identified all the possible outcomes and made a careful estimate of the probability of each outcome. It is not possible to predict what will happen in every case. The most common causes of failure can usually be attributed to a loss of commitment to the project, but there are several others. Part of the planning process entails identifying and addressing these risks.

Loss of Commitment

There are various possible scenarios for loss of commitment. The vendor of a turnkey system may decide to withdraw from the market because of unsatisfactory profit potential or financial difficulties; a library adminstration may alter the budgetary priorities and cut off funding; an in-house computer center may put other customers ahead of the library in its development or operating schedule; or some staff may resist automation, while the rest may withdraw support to avoid conflict.

A number of examples can be cited. The Princeton University Library contracted with the 3M Company, a multibillion-dollar corporation, for the design and installation of an automated circulation control system. A year after the system was installed, the company withdrew from the automated library systems market because the development costs were much greater than expected and alternative products were deemed potentially more profitable. The Denison Memorial Library at University of Colorado Medical Center developed, programmed and tested an automated circulation system and then was informed that no computer time was available for running the system.[1] A number of years ago, the University of Utah Library was encouraged by a computer center with a great deal of unused machine time to develop an automated monographs acquisition system. But when demands on the system increased, library tasks were given a lower priority than those submitted by the University's research faculty.[2]

Ralph McCoy, a pioneer in circulation automation, warned as long ago as 1965, "People at university computer centers are generally oriented toward scientific and research users and in a tight situation will give the library's needs second priority.... [A] library needs more than the expressed sympathy of those who control the computer equipment—it needs firm commitments."[3] And Allen Veaner, for many years associated with Stanford University's BALLOTS effort, which became the basis of the Research Libraries Information Network (RLIN), did a study of 24 institutions' academic computing facilities and concluded that "the facilities were always being taken apart and put back together again."[4]

Public libraries, too, have had unfortunate experiences with automation. A West Coast public library automated when "free" machine time became available on the municipal computer. A year later service fees were announced. Because the municipality would not increase the library budget to pay the fees, the library had to make painful cuts in other areas of its budget.

Inadequate Resources

Efforts to develop in-house integrated library systems involve the greatest risks. After beginning automation, a library may realize too late that it lacks the human and financial resources to complete the project. For example, a highly sophisticated Florida Atlantic University project, begun in 1968, proved to be too much for that institution and had to be abandoned. The first Northwestern On-line Total Integrated System (NOTIS) was designed for Northwestern University's library system at considerable cost but was never made operational. The second NOTIS system had a life span of seven years before being replaced by NOTIS 3.[5] Northwestern's experience parallels that of many business' electronic data processing (EDP) departments, which spend more than half their time modifying existing systems. Fortunately, Northwestern University's support never flagged. Automated systems are dynamic, and constant outlays must be made to adapt them to changing needs and technologies.

Organizational Changes

One of the least frequently mentioned risks of automation is the impact on a library's organization. The organizational and procedural changes necessary to adopt the Online Computer Library Center, Inc. (OCLC) system in one research library were documented in a detailed article by D. Kaye Gapen and Ichiko T. Morita[6] of Ohio State University. Studies show that the traditional library organizational structure is built around files; without the files, units begin to disappear, and the organization chart shrinks.

Gunther Pflug's comments on the side effects of automation, though made several years ago, are still relevant:

> In a conventional library the departments are largely autonomous. The establishment and modification of work processes usually affect merely the department in which such changes are to be carried out.... Nearly all library automation projects, which have been put into effect until now, have left the library's organizational pattern untouched.... In only a few cases have integrated systems, in the narrow meaning of the term, been conceived; still more rarely have steps been undertaken to translate these concepts into reality....
>
> This tying of all departments into a data bank results in considerably stronger interrelatedness between the departments with the effect that, in the interest of reducing friction, the sphere of action of the department heads must be more limited [in libraries with integrated systems] than in conventional libraries. In an integrated automated system, organizational decisions, which up to now could be handled on the departmental level, will become the responsibility of the top administrative level of the library.

Pflug went on to say that day-to-day decisions in this environment are "fraught with a considerably higher risk."[7]

Henry C. Lucas Jr. has also stressed the risks of automation, citing the differences between introducing an automated process and revising the manual process.[8]

Staff Resistance

There is little evidence that libraries have reduced the sizes of their staffs as the result of automation. A few reassignments have apparently occurred, but no layoffs can be documented except for a dramatic reduction in the number of electronic data processing specialists on the staff of the Cleveland Public Library when an in-house system was replaced by a turnkey system. The number of positions in the library's data processing office was reduced from ten to two, and most of the EDP specialists lacked the library background to be reassigned to other jobs.[9]

Nonetheless, staff resistance to change has been mentioned by several library managers as a significant if unmeasurable factor in the automation of a library. That resistance, which may be unconscious rather than conscious, can often be overcome by carefully outlining the perceived benefits of the automation program and by reassuring people regularly. Visiting libraries that have successfully automated appears to be another effective way of dealing with psychological obstacles to automation. Warren J. Haas of the Council on Library Resources puts it this way: "People are protective of what they have built and have gotten to know. Accept that as a given. Don't ignore it."[10]

Patron Attitudes

A number of libraries have experienced system reliability problems when first beginning to operate an automated library system and thus received sharp criticisms from the patrons. Conflicts then developed between those staff members who had opposed automation and those who had favored it, and many who had been supportive withdrew their encouragement when under pressure. An administrator in one library now carries the following quotation in her purse:

> The innovator makes enemies of all those who prospered under the old order and only lukewarm support is forthcoming from those who would prosper under the new. Their support is lukewarm partly from fear of their adversaries who have existing laws on their side, and partly, because men are generally incredulous, never really trusting new things unless they have tested them by experience.[11]

Fear of Failure

Another risk of automation is fear of failure. One library administrator candidly admitted to feeling that it was not worth endangering a reputation built over many years by a decision for which there are no guaranteed results.

Thomas J. Galvin of the Graduate School of Library and Information Sciences at the University of Pittsburgh formulated the best response to this view, "The manager who makes fewer mistakes may actually be declining in managerial effectiveness and sidestepping or avoiding the very adminstrative and supervisory responsibilities [that] are, or ought to be, the essential content of his or her work."[12]

Some of the risks and failures described in this chapter could have been avoided or lessened by more careful planning; others could not. Nonetheless, a well conceived plan, rigorously adhered to, still offers the best chance of success. Automation is not for the impulsive.

THE VALUE OF PLANNING

Planning is time-consuming, but it is usually cost-effective because time spent planning will reduce the time required later for system implementation. Even when several people participate in planning for a number of months, the total number of hours they work will be less than the amount of time a much larger number of people will commit to implementing and operating a new system in the first few months after installation.

Planning is an effort to formulate a proposal for future activity. The key to the success of any automation program is the systematic selecting and relating of facts to a number of assumptions about the future. The futuristic aspect of planning is what makes it an uncomfortable undertaking. Managers are hesitant to predict future events given only limited data. However, the alternative to planning is random movement or a series of reactions to external influences. Without planning there is no means of control after implementation has begun.

THE PLANNING PROCESS

Good planning is usually formal and recorded in writing, but it can be informal and oral. The essential ingredient in planning is a systematic procedure that has several components: problem definition, analysis, synthesis, evaluation and iteration.

Defining the Problem or Need

In the first step of the planning process, the role of the manager is critical. It is the manager who should spell out the purpose of this particular planning phase: its scope, the amount of time available for the study, the budget and who is to be in charge. Some expert advice will be needed at this stage. An in-house systems analyst or an outside consultant can provide some guidance about what is feasible and the time required to plan and implement a system. The analyst or consultant can also be charged with actually writing the problem statement or definition of needs. If, however, a draft is written by someone who has limited training in analysis, it should be subjected to a critique by an analyst or consultant. Key staff should be involved in extensive discussion of the statement so that errors can be corrected and differences of opinion reconciled. The outcome of this first step should be a clear statement of the problem or need.

It is obvious that the library manager should seek the approval of the next higher level of management when he or she is satisfied that the definition of the problem or task has been adequately formulated; however, this is often not done after the initial go-ahead. Management commitment—both financial and personal—is essential to automating and should be sought again whenever there is a significant change in direction or scope of planning. The manager should be particularly careful to repeat the review of this step with new presidents, provosts, library boards or superintendents who may be appointed during the life of the project. Commitments are both personal and institutional, and the latter are often shaped by the former.

It is important to stress at this stage that approval is not being sought to automate, but to address an identified problem or need: cost reduction, service improvement, records control, resource sharing with other institutions or a combination of these.

As soon as approval has been secured, the library manager should appoint a senior staff member as project coordinator—someone who has the time to do the job properly. It is more important that the individual have a good management record, rather than a great deal of knowledge about specific library activities. It is far easier to acquire information than it is to learn good management skills and attitudes.

Analyzing Operations

The next task is to analyze the library's operations. It is this step that is usually shortcut by those who are already convinced that the present manual procedures are not working and that automation is the answer. The lack of detailed information about manual operations is also responsible for the lack of cost comparisons between manual and automated library systems. One must be careful to identify the problem, not the symptoms.

For example, a library with a problem checking in serials decided it had to automate to eliminate backlogs in checkin and claiming. The manual kardex records were reviewed and corrected to prepare them for conversion to machine-readable form. Even before the automated system was installed, both functions were current because the cleaned-up kardex records dramatically improved the productivity of the staff.

The library literature is filled with articles detailing techniques for analysis of library operations and costs, but there have been very few cost studies. Ohio State University undertook a pilot cost study, which documented an increase from a "basic unit cost" per title for cataloging from $8.30 in 1970 to $11.11 in 1975, after implementing OCLC shared cataloging. In real dollars, or dollars adjusted for inflation, that represented a decrease of 40 cents from 1970 to 1975.[13] As of mid-1983, no full-fledged study has been published that would provide detailed, reliable information.

The price for a good cost study can be very high—up to $40,000 for a whole library and up to $10,000 for the study of a single function. There is no point in undertaking such a study if the decision to proceed with automation is going to be based substantially on other factors, such as service improvements and the availability of better management information.[14] A library may use generalized data to develop its conclusions, rather than data drawn from an analysis of its own specific operations. The *Annual Review of Information Science and Technology* (published by Knowledge Industry Publications, Inc. for the American Society for Information Science) is an excellent source for up-to-date bibliographies on automation and related technologies.

Synthesis

The examination of alternatives quickly reveals options that go beyond the automation of existing activities. It is not just a matter of performing the same tasks more quickly or more economically. Significant service and management improvements can be realized by automating. A circulation system, for example, can become a powerful public inquiry system, and circulation statistics can provide vital management information for collection development.

At this point in the study, the library should go back to the beginning. It is likely that the original problem definition was not formulated in terms as broad as those the available automation options allow. The advantage of a formal, systematic planning process is that it may keep a library from rushing ahead before the first step has been reexamined. Successful planning is more likely if the library manager and the project coordinator keep the process clearly in mind and are not overwhelmed by dozens of pages of reports. It is the library manager who must decide, in consultation with higher management and the staff, whether to adhere to the problem statement as originally formulated, to curtail it or to expand it.

The most common example of a change in the problem or needs statement occurs when a library manager has authorized planning for an improved circulation system and is told that some of the vendors of turnkey online systems offer low-cost automated circulation systems, while other vendors offer more costly, larger systems that are designed to be integrated library systems supporting several functions sharing a common data base. The budgetary constraints and current library needs may suggest adherence to the initial plan, but a review may result in a longer-term view and a broader mandate.

Evaluation and Iteration

At this stage in the planning process, the library should develop detailed specifications or requirements, which will enable it to evaluate all alternatives for automation. The specifications should outline expected performance, rather than specific methods. Ideally, the library should write its own specifications, rather than relying on a consultant or on specifications obtained from another library. Although more time consuming, this approach is the surest way to reflect the needs of the library accurately and to get the interest and commitment of the staff who must later work with the system. It is, however, worthwhile to retain a consultant to review the specifications for possible inconsistencies and oversights.

Evaluation of automation alternatives will be aided if elements in the specifications are weighted or labeled "must," "highly desirable" and "desirable" at the outset. Again, these priorities should reflect the decisions made in the definition of the problem. If they do not, that first step should be repeated.

COOPERATIVE VENTURES

An alternative to planning for automation by individual libraries is cooperative planning among several libraries in a community or even in an entire state. Such planning may be done by a multi-type library group or by libraries that are all of the same type. Cooperative planning may or may not involve cooperative implementation. Much data gathering, analysis and specification development can be shared, yet separate systems purchased.

Joint Planning

The advantages of cooperative ventures to automate can include less risk, more systematic planning, the ability to draw on a number of people with a wide range of expertise, lower planning cost per institution and greater sensitivity to the future linking or networking of the computer systems in the various libraries. The principal drawbacks of cooperative planning are that a longer time period is required for planning and implementation and that it may be an uncomfortable experience. A participating institution is likely to be challenged on many of its policies and procedures by other libraries in a consortium.

Barbara E. Markuson, director of the Indiana Cooperative Library Services Authority (INCOLSA), said: "All technology carries an element of risk. [A network] can take risks. Individual libraries can't. They can spread the risks over many libraries."[15] This is particularly important in the case of cataloging, because a large computer system is involved, but even smaller ventures can be less risky when undertaken together. Offsetting the greater safety of cooperative ventures is the slower pace that is usually associated with negotiating solutions so that they will be acceptable to all of the participants.

There are several examples of successful cooperative planning, including the joint venture of the libraries of the Miami Valley of Ohio in early 1979 and the CONSUL libraries of New England in 1982. The five Miami Valley libraries, both public and academic, developed a request for proposal (RFP), committed funds and sought bids for an outside consulting team to undertake a good deal of the planning.

The RFP called for an evaluation of the existing circulation systems of the five libraries to determine their efficiency and how well they met the goals and objectives of the institutions. It also ordered a comparison of the present circulation systems with automated systems, both in terms of costs and advantages and disadvantages. Other requirements were to determine the value and cost of a cooperative circulation system, as compared with individual systems, and to recommend whether or not each library should retain its present system or automate.

A second phase of the evaluation required the development of a model for a computerized circulation system and a recommendation for data conversion. Evaluation of existing turnkey systems against the model was also specified. Finally, preparation of an RFP to solicit bids from qualified vendors of automated circulation systems was sought. The cost to the libraries for all of the above was less than $5000 per library.

CONSUL is comprised of the six state-supported university libraries of New England. The group retained a consulting firm in 1982 and had it determine the local needs of the six libraries and what, if any, linkages were desirable among the systems. No cooperative automation project was undertaken, but each institution had its needs assessed and was provided with a suitable set of specifications for procurement of its system. One aspect of the specifications was provision for dial up into one another's systems.

The amount of cooperative planning is increasing. In the past three years more than two dozen joint studies have been undertaken in the United States, some of them involving more than 50 libraries.

Cooperative Systems in Operation

One of the most effective ways to limit the capital costs of automating is by jointly acquiring a turnkey system. Libraries can share the cost of the CPU and the software and at the same time have the benefit of a system's extended holdings. There already are such cooperative efforts in states as widely scattered as Connecticut, Illinois, Utah and Alaska.

The Connecticut State Library conducted a demonstration of a CL Systems, Inc. (CLSI) turnkey circulation system as early as August 1973. Its intent was to have several libraries make a joint solicitation for a study of the potential, immediate applications of online computer technology in Connecticut libraries. The study was delayed, but three years later a shared system was actually installed.

Additional clusters of libraries undertook similar joint ventures in the mid-1970s. Recognizing the interlibrary loan potential of several automated circulation control systems in the state, the Illinois State Library appointed a standards committee to develop guidelines for bibliographic entries. The State Library also offered $25,000 grants from its Library Services and Construction Act (LSCA) funds to all cluster library systems that would cooperate in an effort to link data bases. Simple dial-up equipment in the State Library made it possible to display the contents of the data bases of the Suburban and North Suburban Library Systems and the Rockford Public Library on a CRT. Subsequent installations of dial-up equipment were made in the other libraries. Each library was then scheduled to call each other daily and did so regularly for several years. Consequently, more than four titles per minute could be searched, including the recording of the location symbol and call number. In 1982, electronic linkages were established among the systems to facilitate searching.

One of the significant discoveries made in Illinois was that with a large number of unique titles listed in each data base, the availability of materials can be quickly confirmed. In addition, patrons can be very quickly "blocked" or "trapped" in all of the cooperating libraries, so that a delinquent borrower cannot take out additional materials.

The initial efforts in Illinois libraries were limited only by the capacity of the small CPU employed. In early 1978, four CPUs were required to support 39 terminals. Most turnkey system vendors are now offering systems with the capability of handling this many terminals on a single CPU. Super-minis can accommodate as many as 90 multiprocessor systems and are theoretically capable of handling several hundred terminals.

The Illinois libraries had the advantage of state support for their library systems, but the costs of automation were borne fully by the individual libraries. Staff support at the system level played a major role at various stages of planning and implementation, but there may have been too little participation by the staffs of the various libraries. A pioneering effort is not always a model effort. This is why future cooperative ventures should be based on a review of several earlier efforts.

USING CONSULTANTS

Both individual and cooperative planning efforts can often be improved by using outside consultants to assure objective, formal planning in a short time and at a known and moderate cost. Consulting services cost from $250 to $500 per day plus expenses, but when used effectively, they will save several times that amount for the library.

James D. Lockwood, former head of reference at Indiana University Law Library, has listed the advantages that consultants provide:

- A source of new ideas and/or fresh approaches

- Analytical ability

- Specialized skills and experience

- Superior ability to introduce and implement change

- Ability to work on a specific problem with all of his/her resources at one time

- Objectivity

- More up-to-date knowledge than that of library staff[16]

The American Library Association and state library agencies are good sources of names of consultants. Also see Appendix A of this book.

But using consultants also has the possible disadvantage of insufficiently involving the library manager and staff in the consultation process. A responsible consultant will insist on such involvement, but since consultants charge by the hour, most libraries are forced to place strict limits on the number of days devoted to staff-consultant meetings. A consultant will normally seek to formalize the planning process and gain prior agreement on the role of the library manager and the appointment of a project coordinator.

A library or group of libraries has the option of appointing its own planning team. Usually such a team will devote only part of its time to the planning process and may have to spend a great deal of that time gathering information already available to an experienced consultant. The time required to complete planning thus becomes longer. The true cost is seldom calculated because people's salaries are existing line items in the general library budget; however, the impact on the operations budget is normally small. The greatest advantage of this approach is that a nucleus of knowledgeable people develops within the library itself.

An in-house team studying automation may not insist on the formality usually associated with a contracted outside study. The group may go to work with a vague responsibility and fail in its mission; even the most competent team can be handicapped by a problem statement that fails to make the objective clear. Therefore, it is a good idea for the library manager to meet with the planners, have them restate the objective(s) and then have some discussion.

IMPLEMENTATION

Once the decision has been made to automate the library, an appropriate computer system must be procured. To do this, the normal process is the release of specifications (or "specs") with a Request for Proposals (RFP). As noted previously, a library should develop its own specifications in order to have them accurately reflect its needs. Several people should participate in preparing and/or reviewing the specifications. This is a way of encouraging the interest and commitment of the library staff members who will have to operate the system after it is installed.

The Request for Proposals

Preparing a set of specifications and the related procurement documents, which together make up the RFP, is fundamental to implementing automation. Even the very largest institutions have been known to generate deplorable documents that make evaluation impossible and bidding a game of roulette for the vendors. There are some simple rules for preparing the specifications and related RFP documents.

1. Explain what is to be automated, in simple, everyday language.

2. Describe the library's present holdings, volume of activities, number of service points and related details so that the vendor can determine what size computer system is required.

3. Estimate the probable growth of the library over the anticipated life of the system so the vendor can determine the probable maximum size of the computer system.

4. Specify any standards that are important to the library, such as the capability to load, retain and output full-MARC bibliographic records.

5. Define any related services the vendor is to supply, either of a basic or optional nature, such as training, staff manuals, labels, etc.

6. Last but not least, tell the vendor how the price or prices should be quoted, and what guarantees or bonding will be required.

Although this is a very simplified list for a document that can run hundreds of pages, these elements are basic to any specification or RFP.

Performance Specifications

The specifications need not be detailed nuts-and-bolts statements that spell out how the computer system shall be designed. A performance specification—one that outlines what the system must be capable of doing—is preferable. It usually assures competitive bidding, because there is greater similarity in the functioning of various systems than in their hardware/software design.

A performance specification may not protect the library against a system design that lacks flexibility for future growth or modification or one that may be costly to expand. The vendor may bid the smallest system capable of meeting the requirements, forcing the library into premature upgrades. The library should, therefore, specify the minimum initial capacity and expandability of the central processor or include in the performance specifications a requirement that the initial system be capable of supporting a specified number of terminals and level of activity. The same should be done for secondary storage. It is far more costly to expand a system designed around small disk drives than one which uses the largest disk drives justified by the size of the library's collection.

There is a problem in setting minimums: vendors may not believe them. One vendor observed:

> ...Libraries do not mean what they say in their specifications. A check of more than a dozen recent contract awards confirms that the lowest bidder is successful far more often than the firm which bids the specifications exactly. A library is usually prepared to sacrifice some features it considers attractive, but not essential, to save a few thousand dollars.[17]

Libraries should decide which features are mandatory before seeking bids and should seek to adhere to the requirements. The mandatory elements can be identified in the specification or retained as a checklist. Some libraries have developed weighted criteria to assist them in evaluating vendor's bids. Such criteria may include:

- Compliance with the specifications

- Expandability

- Flexibility

- Transportability of software

- Interfaces

- Delivery schedule

- Vendor size and past performance

- Total cost of the system over five years

Compliance usually represents half the weight, and the other criteria 10% each. Point counting is not recommended because the best choice is usually one that involves a good balance of all elements, rather than high scores on a few points and poor scores on others. The latter can result in a high overall score but, potentially, the procurement of a system that is basically unattractive.

CONTRACTING WITH A VENDOR

Responses to requests for bids are seldom so complete and clear that a library is left with no unanswered questions. A single person or small team should represent the library in discussions or negotiations with the bidders to determine the answers to these remaining questions. Representations made in these conferences or other oral communications often are not binding, however, unless subsequently written into a contract. The written contract and a limited number of other written documents identified in the contract usually represent the entire agreement between the parties. Consequently, a library should consider retaining an experienced consultant during the evaluation and post-bid negotiation. The vendors are experienced in bidding and in the discussion or negotiations that follow, but few librarians are. A good consultant can provide both technical expertise and observations on the deficiencies of a vendor's contract.

System Description and Performance Standards

The contract should include a detailed system description and an itemization of all the performance standards the vendor has agreed to meet. The library must be careful to ascertain any points of difference between its own specifications and those of the vendor's bids and the final contract. The delivery schedule should also be part of the contract. This means not only the date for the initial delivery of the hardware, but also the timing of the delivery of all software and the demonstration that all contracted functions can be performed. The library should recognize that delivery may take several weeks or months.

Site Preparation

Site preparation for the automated system is usually the library's responsibility and should begin as soon as the contract with the vendor is signed. It is a good idea to obtain detailed, written requirements for the site from the vendor during the negotiation process and to seek a guarantee that a site meeting these characteristics will be acceptable to the vendor. Any future site modifications made necessary because of an error by the vendor or a change in the requirements of the hardware should be decreed in the contract as the responsibility of the vendor.

Terms of Payment

The terms of payment should also be included in the contract. A vendor wants a substantial payment upon signing because up to 40% of the cost of the contract may represent hardware the vendor has to purchase from manufacturers some time before delivery and installation. Payment of substantially more than half, however, may weaken the future negotiating position of the library. The final payment to be made on acceptance of the system should be significant—more than the 20% that is common in many contracts.

Acceptance Tests

An acceptance test plan should be included in the contract. The acceptance test should be a record of consistent performance for a period of at least 30 days of all functions specified. Although 100% performance is rarely achieved, the CPU should be functioning 98% to 99% of the time, and the entire system should achieve almost that high a level of performance.

Hardware and Software Maintenance

The contract also should clearly spell out the terms of the maintenance program for both hardware and software. Hardware maintenance is usually done by the manufacturer(s), although at least one major turnkey system vendor (CLSI) has sought to do all maintenance itself. The important points are to determine that a service representative is available nearby and that this representative has access to a local stock of parts.

Software maintenance may be limited to remedying any defects that are discovered after the system has been installed and accepted, or it may include software improvements made to the vendor's standard system. The latter benefits the library by providing a dynamic system that can accommodate the constantly changing improvements in library automation. The vendor also benefits because it has to support only a single standard system rather than many different systems.

STAFF TRAINING

Preliminary training should begin shortly after the contract is signed, when curiosity is usually high. The training itself has several components. Initially, it should consist of a basic orientation to the system, as well as demonstrations of what the system will do and how it will affect the duties of the staff and services to the users of the library. Good publicity at this stage can play an important role in winning staff acceptance of the new system.

Most initial training in the use of turnkey systems is done by representatives of the vendors. A few libraries have chosen to have a small number of people trained by the vendors and to have these people, in turn, train the rest of the staff. Libraries that have done this appear to have better ongoing training programs. Turnover in libraries can be high, especially among clerical personnel in public libraries and student employees in academic libraries. Also, there are usually a few new people who must be made familiar with the equipment. The author has visited numerous libraries with automated systems and observed serious misuse and abuse of light pens, CRT terminals and printers because the staff was inadequately trained. It is a good idea to designate a particular staff member to train new employees and to periodically retrain the others.

RECORDS CONVERSION

Converting the library's collection of old manual or machine-readable records, or both, should be undertaken as early as possible because it is usually a time-consuming task. There are strong differences of opinion on how much of a library's data base must be developed before a system can be effectively used. As noted in Chapter 5, in the case of circulation systems, converting 50% of the data is considered a minimum for most public libraries. The figure is usually higher for special libraries and lower for academic libraries. For an online catalog, 100% conversion beginning with a specific imprint date is considered best by many experts.

Chapter 5 included a detailed discussion of alternative sources for retrospective conversion support. Three primary methods are briefly reviewed here.

The least expensive method is "conversion-on-the-fly," in which a new machine-readable record is created only when the item or old record is being handled for another specific purpose. In this manner, years may pass before all of the file is converted. This approach has been popular, especially with very large libraries. However, libraries are increasingly relying on large bibliographic data bases available from commercial vendors. Such a large machine-readable data base can be loaded in the system and the file searched for records that match the local manual or incomplete machine-readable records. All of those that match, or are "hits," can then be incorporated into the new data base. However, unless the capacity of the computer system is great enough to accommodate the temporary loading of the large data base, response time will be very poor, and poor response time can appreciably increase the labor costs of conversion.

A third approach is to send the library's records to a commercial firm that specializes in data conversion. Although this is usually the most expensive approach, it is quick, there is often greater quality control, and the library is protected against unexpected costs. Also, the library may provide a microfilm of the shelflist or, to save money, may submit an abbreviated record typed on optical character recognition (OCR) equipment. The latter is normally used for machine scanning and matching against the vendor's data base.

Competitive bidding is strongly recommended for large conversion projects because prices vary a great deal.

SELLING THE PROGRAM

Investing in a technologically sound system does not assure success. Similar libraries, installing identical automation systems, can have widely differing results, depending on staff and user reactions. The library that is constantly encountering problems with staff and users is usually the one that lacks a planned program of promoting the new system. Furthermore, the library that carefully identifies all of the groups that are—or should be—interested in the new automated system and informs them of what is happening has greater acceptance and apparently fewer problems.

A single promotional technique is not sufficient. Moreover, different "audiences" may require different information or emphases. Staff members are probably most interested in knowing how an automated system can relieve them of routine chores. Patrons, on the other hand, may be more concerned about how the system will save them time or improve access to information. Finally, adminstrators may wish to learn the ways in which improved management information will result in more effective use of library resources.

Although a library manager's personal contacts may be the most effective way to sell the new automated system, those contacts will be limited by the time available. Libraries have employed a variety of other techniques, both to announce plans to automate and to report progress on installation and operation.

Newspaper Stories

Articles in a community, campus or company newspaper describing the library's automation program have been the most common promotion technique used with large groups, but success has been mixed. Several libraries lost control over the stories because the newspaper reporter took the initiative and developed a story on the basis of a few telephone interviews. Unplanned interviews can produce the wrong emphasis or sometimes actual misinformation. To avoid these problems, a press release that carefully describes what the library wishes to say is essential. The release should be interesting, even at the risk of leaving out details; the expository material may be covered by a manual or leaflet.

Leaflet

A handout describing the why, when and how of a new library automation system is inexpensive and effective. It can be aimed at those who most use the library. Although the leaflet should emphasize the prospective benefits to the library user, it should also set forth any possible disadvantages. It is tempting to oversell when a library feels its audience may be unsure or skeptical about an innovation, but the problems created if the automation timetable is delayed may be fatal to the entire program. For example, when one public library had to discontinue use of its new circulation system for several weeks to iron out some reliability problems, it reportedly had significant difficulties explaining the delay to a public that had come to expect great things from the heavily promoted system.

Staff Newsletter

Eli Oboler has advocated that a staff bulletin can be "the most common and important single regular publication of a library with more than five employees. It need not be...elaborate...but it does need to be an honest and thorough report of what is going on in the library."[18] The bulletin can have an effect beyond that of helping employees to formulate their own opinions. Its influence can be transmitted, in turn, to the hundreds of users with whom the staff is in daily contact. The newsletter is an effective ongoing way of telling the story of a new automated system.

Radio

A few libraries have arranged interviews on campus or publicly supported community radio stations. This somewhat more personal identification with the interviewee can result in greater acceptance and more response than are generated by a printed story.

Displays

Public libraries have made the greatest use of promotional displays. Simple explanations of how the computer system works are of particular interest. Photographs of the various components of the system in use are inexpensive and can also be used for newspaper and newsletter stories.

Demonstrations

Demonstrations of the computer system for the staff should be done even before the system is installed. (A good demonstration is more convincing than the best of prose.) Also, rehearsing with the staff is essential to avoid damaging mistakes. It is important that everyone be able to see clearly. CRT displays can be presented on a large screen television receiver borrowed or rented for the occasion. If no large screen display is available, only very small groups, ideally six people or fewer, are advisable.

Public demonstrations can also be scheduled. The Princeton University Library placed a patron record conversion station in the main lobby outside the circulation desk and found that the terminal operator drew a curious and appreciative crowd all day long.

Support Groups

The friends of the public library or the campus or company library committee can be an important supporting group from the earliest planning stage through implementation of a computer system, even when the statutory responsibility is limited. The people composing such groups usually have quite diverse interests and thus will pose the questions on the minds of many library users. They can also be a source of sympathetic support when the computer system malfunctions.

Contacts with Opinion Leaders

The library's manager and staff have usually identified the people who most influence opinion in their community, company or academic organization. A letter to each of these people describing the new program can be very effective. Personal contacts, when possible, are even better. The approach should be informational rather than promotional and ideally should be made just before a newspaper story is scheduled to appear. People who influence the opinions of others do so because they usually have news before everyone else.

Remedial Activity

At times, even the best of automation systems will frustrate some library users. For example, a record may be temporarily lost, or two different records may be tied together. A phone call to someone who has had difficulty with the library's new system can keep the library manager and immediate staff alert to progress and might prevent the individual from broadcasting the problem. Staff should be instructed to record the names of patrons who were inconvenienced so that the follow-up can be made.

All of the foregoing techniques are already being used by many public libraries as part of their ongoing efforts to promote the library as a whole. They are less common in academic and special libraries. The higher risks associated with introducing automated systems make such efforts particularly important.

SUMMARY

The use of a planning process to automate can be time-consuming, costly and sometimes annoying; but it will produce fewer unwelcome surprises later. Like most major changes, automation is not without risks, but careful planning can reduce if not eliminate the possibilities for failure.

There is a middle ground between detailed planning, as outlined in some of the literature, and the lack of systematic planning that has occurred in many libraries. An effective compromise is to use the planning outline as a structure, without doing all of the detailed data gathering that takes so much time and money. The planning process often works almost as well with rough estimates as with exact figures. It protects a library against serious omissions, which is much more important than predicting costs to within 10%.

Cooperative planning is another way of lowering costs for individual libraries. Such ventures have been undertaken by both public and academic libraries in many regions of the United States. Consultants can be extremely useful to both groups and individual libraries that are engaged in planning for automation.

Once again, it is the library manager's responsibility to make the final decision(s), after weighing costs versus service effectiveness. Staff members must be involved in the planning process, and the reasons for the final decision to automate must be understood and supported by them and by higher-level management.

Once the decision to automate has been made, there are two basic aspects in carrying it out: first, procuring and starting up the system, and second, selling the program to the library staff and patrons.

Procurement starts with a performance specification, drawn up by the library, which may then be submitted to vendors for competitive bids. Evaluation of bids and contract negotiations, often with the aid of a consultant, constitute the next step. The final contract should include a detailed system description (with a list of all performance standards to be met by the vendor), the delivery schedule, site requirements, terms of payment, an acceptance test plan and terms of the maintenance program for both hardware and software.

Conversion should be undertaken as soon as possible; large conversion projects necessitate competitive bidding and evaluation even before the computer system is selected. Training the staff to use the automated system should begin as soon as the contract is signed. It also seems advisable to have some library staff members trained by the vendor so that they, in turn, can maintain ongoing training programs for employees.

Promoting the new system is crucial to successful implementation. Effective promotional techniques include newspaper articles, staff newsletters, leaflets, radio interviews, displays and demonstrations for the staff and the public. Community leaders and library support groups should also be included in the library's promotional effort.

Chapter 8 looks at future trends in library automation.

FOOTNOTES

1. Irwin H. Pizer, "Planning to Implementation; the Problems en Route," *Bulletin of the Medical Library Association*, January 1976, pp. 2-3.

2. Related to the author by a former systems analyst at the institution.

3. Ralph E. McCoy, "Computerized Circulation Work: A Case Study of the 357 Data Collection System," *Library Resources and Technical Services*, Winter 1965, pp. 59-65.

4. Personal communication with the author.

5. Karen L. Horney, "NOTIS-3...," *Library Resources and Technical Services*, Fall 1978, pp. 361-367.

6. D. Kaye Gapen and Ichiko T. Morita, "OCLC at OSU: The Effect of the Adoption of OCLC on the Management of Technical Services at a Large Academic Library," *Library Resources and Technical Services*, Winter 1978, pp. 5-21.

7. Gunther Pflug, "Effects of Automation on Library Adminstration," *Library Association Journal* 14 (1975), pp. 271-272

8. Henry C. Lucas Jr., *Information Systems Concepts for Managers* (New York: McGraw-Hill Book Co., 1977).

9. James M. O'Brien, former technical services head of the Cleveland Public Library, in telephone conversation with the author, January 23, 1979.

10. Warren J. Haas, speech at the Association of College and Research Libraries Meeting, Boston, November 8, 1978. For an edited transcript, see *College and Research Libraries*, March 1979, pp. 109-119.

11. Niccolo Machiavelli, *The Prince* (London: Folio Society, 1970).

12. Thomas J. Galvin, "Management in Interesting Times," keynote address at the 1978 Army Library Institute, El Paso, TX, May 22, 1978.

13. D. Kaye Gapen and Ichiko T. Morita, "A Cost Analysis of the Ohio College Library Center On-Line Shared Cataloging System in the Ohio State University Libraries," *Library Resources and Technical Services*, Summer 1977, pp. 286-301.

14. For ideas, consult Geoffrey Ford, *Library Automation: Guidelines to Costing* (Wetherby, England: British Library Lending Division, 1973, ED 082-757.)

15. Barbara E. Markuson, speech at Association of College and Research Libraries Meeting, Boston, November 10, 1978. For an edited transcript see *College and Research Libraries*, March 1979, pp. 125-135.

16. James D. Lockwood, "Involving Consultants in Library Change," *College and Research Libraries*, November 1977, pp. 498-508.

17. Richard Boss, "Circulation Systems: The Options," *Library Technology Reports*, January/ February 1979, p. 81.

18. Eli M. Oboler, "Selling the Academic Library," *Public Relations for Libraries* (Westport, CT: Greenwood Press, 1973), p. 147.

8

Future Trends

Automated systems and new communications technologies are profoundly affecting library services and the role of the library manager. The revolution has been under way for some time, and there is every indication that it will accelerate in the second half of the 1980s. Modern library managers must be aware of current options. Further, they should be alert to developing trends and their potential impact on the future of the library.

This chapter will comment on the changes that are occurring in library automation, including the trend toward integrated systems, the role of bibliographic utilities and the growing importance of remote data base searching. It will also survey emerging technologies such as videotext, video and optical digital discs, electronic mail, digital telefacsimile, and the use of satellite or fiber optic systems as alternatives to telephone and cable communications.

AUTOMATION TRENDS

Dramatic changes in library automation have occurred since the 1960s, when the University of Chicago, Northwestern University, Stanford University and the University of Toronto all launched pioneering efforts to develop online integrated computerized systems that would support all library functions from preorder searching through to the circulation of materials. Each of these systems was designed around a large mainframe computer at a cost of millions of dollars. The institutions originally envisioned the replication of their in-house systems by other libraries. Recently, however, they have sought to extend the in-house systems to other libraries by networking or sale of software to provide a broader basis of financial support for their own ongoing software development.

The integrated or total systems approach, in which a single bibliographic file supports all functions—acquisitions, serials, cataloging, circulation, etc.—is philosophically and technically sound. Only one input or update needs to be performed to keep the entire data base current for all functions, and only one query needs to be made to search the entire data base. However, historically, most institutions rejected this approach in favor of automating only those functions that appeared to lend themselves to rapid and less expensive automation. Hundreds of libraries developed automated acquisitions and circulation systems in the decade from the mid-1960s through the mid-1970s.

It was this market that attracted the commercial vendors. From a single vendor of turnkey or packaged systems in 1974, the market grew to accommodate nine vendors in 1978. By early 1978 the market was so competitive that one firm considering entry concluded that it would "have to virtually give systems away for a year or two to establish a foothold." Between 1978 and 1983, six more vendors entered the turnkey market, but five dropped out. This dramatic pattern of growth is primarily attributable to the availability of low-cost, powerful minicomputers. The commercial vendors were able to purchase hardware, develop software packages, and market and install several systems for less than the cost of a single mainframe computer.

Minicomputer technology will continue to shape the pattern of library automation development for the forseeable future. The large super-minis with 1MB to 6MB of primary memory and new mass storage devices will soon be capable of supporting integrated library systems for entire consortia. A library or consortium need not depend on a large mainframe computer in a data processing center staffed by professional electronic data processing personnel. Sharing systems based on the large minis may not reduce the costs of automating, but it will facilitate resource sharing in local areas. Once the political problems of resource sharing are overcome, libraries can begin to plan their collection development in the light of the collections and acquisitions patterns of other institutions.

The turnkey approach to library automation will probably continue to be dominant. The turnkey stand-alone systems offer a great degree of in-house control over local functions such as circulation and patron access catalogs while spreading the cost of research, development, programming and maintenance of automated systems among many libraries.

As of mid-1983, all of the turnkey systems included circulation control—in most cases extremely sophisticated packages with many tables of options. Acquisitions was available from most vendors, and patron access catalogs were offered by half the vendors. Serials control was under development and generally promised for 1984. Media booking was offered by one vendor—CTI Library Systems, Inc.—and three others had it under active development. Authority control was beginning to be developed in response to libraries' demands for improved data base creation and maintenance capabilities and more sophisticated searching routines. The development of future functions will also depend on vendor perception of demand.

It is imperative that a library's initial procurement decision anticipate these trends and take them into consideration. A system selected to serve only one library in the performance of a limited range of functions may need to be expanded to support additional libraries and/or the automation of additional functions; this has implications for the selection of hardware and software. In choosing the turnkey system and in selecting from the different central processing units (CPUs) supported by a vendor, a library can address the potential need for expandability in a number of ways. It may decide to acquire the largest available CPU or to begin with a smaller unit to meet its immediate needs, stipulating that the CPU be capable of being upgraded without requiring the replacement of anything already acquired; it may select a software package that is "transportable," or hardware-independent; or it may select a system that offers a multiprocessor configuration so that other CPUs can be added later.

Potentially even more dramatic than the impact of minicomputers is the emergence of multiuser, multitasking microcomputers. These are a far cry from the so-called personal computers in widespread use. Only 7% of the micros installed by 1983 could accommodate more than one terminal *and* support the accessing of more than one function at a time. The most widely used such micro in libraries was the Digital Equipment Corp. PDP 11/23, a micro that is actually a slimmed-down mini. Both Avatar Systems, Inc. and CL Systems, Inc. (CLSI) were offering systems configured around this machine. CTI, with its highly transportable software based on the Pick operating system, offered both the Datamedia Corp. and Honeywell Information Systems, Inc. Ultimate micros.

At least one company was working on software for the Altos Computer Systems micros in mid-1983. A system configured around this small but powerful micro might be priced at less than $50,000.

BIBLIOGRAPHIC UTILITIES

Shared cataloging networks such as Online Computer Library Center, Inc. (OCLC), Research Libraries Information Network (RLIN), Washington Library Network (WLN), and University of Toronto Library Automation System (UTLAS) will continue to have a major effect on the pattern of development of library automation. OCLC has revenues of more than $40 million a year and the largest research and development staff in librarianship.

By 1983 all of the bibliographic utilities supported not only cataloging but also acquisitions and interlibrary loans. OCLC also offered serials control and a union listing subsystem. None had moved into the area of distributed systems. Only OCLC was known to be actively seeking to move into the local library automation areas of circulation and patron access catalog. It was pursuing the development of a system based on the Integrated Library System software originally developed by the Lister Hill Center for Biomedical Communications of the National Library of Medicine (NLM). OCLC had announced a development agreement with Online Computer Services, Inc., one of the two major vendors offering ILS-based systems, and had entered into negotiation to purchase the second company, Avatar.

All of the utilities were offering retrospective conversion, but only OCLC had turned it into a multimillion dollar service. OCLC not only discounted online retrospective conversion undertaken by libraries in off-hours but also contracted to perform the keying at its facilities.

The bibliographic utilities could be challenged by the distribution of bibliographic data by commercial firms. All the utilities could be adversely affected if a commercial organization were to offer libraries machine-readable bibliographic records in MARC format for loading into stand-alone systems. Such a service could use the economical video disc or optical digital disc as storage and distribution media. In both cases, digitized information would be stored on a plastic disc about 12 inches in diameter and read by a computer-controlled laser. Once a master was made, discs could be stamped at a high speed at costs of less than $2 per million characters. (Video and optical discs will be discussed in more detail later in this chapter.)

The major challenge facing the developer of a commercial bibliographic data service, irrespective of the storage and distribution medium chosen, would be gathering the data. Even the LC MARC tapes contain only half the number of bibliographic records available from a utility. The main asset of the utilities is their comprehensive data bases, made possible by their requirement that participants input all of their original cataloging into the systems. There has apparently been no research to determine the minimum number of contributing libraries that would be needed to build a data base as large as the one created by the 3300 OCLC participants. It might require only a few dozen very large libraries or a well-selected combination of highly specialized libraries. A service that offered a high "hit rate" and good quality records might appeal to libraries with stand-alone systems.

STATE AND REGIONAL NETWORKS

State and regional networks may emerge. In 1983 concern was being expressed by some participants in national planning bodies that some state library agencies might replace their statewide COM catalogs with online data bases that could be used by local libraries to support cataloging and retrospective conversion. It was feared that this could reduce the revenue of the utilities and possibly place these local library records beyond the reach of libraries in other areas.

The fears appeared to be ill-founded. The author surveyed all 50 state library agencies in 1983 and determined that only one-fourth planned to support the development of state-wide or regional data bases. In most cases these plans were for small states that envisioned the sharing of multifunction turnkey systems among major libraries, much as consortia in other states have done on a local level. Two states foresaw only the creation of data bases of brief records to support interlibrary lending.

In only two states was there an active effort to create a statewide online data base that could be used in lieu of a bibliographic utility for cataloging support. The majority of the state library agencies planned to continue their COM catalogs for interlibrary loan (ILL) locations, envisioning the continued use of the ILL subsystems of the utilities, or anticipated the linkage of several of the turnkey systems in their states.

COMPUTER-TO-COMPUTER COMMUNICATIONS

The 1977 study on interfaces conducted under the auspices of the National Commission on Libraries and Information Science has had virtually no effect on the development of interfaces among local systems. While the technical constraints are few, there is little likelihood that competing vendors will coordinate their design efforts to permit easy communication among systems. Nor do libraries appear to be placing a high priority on computer-to-computer communication. Most specifications call for the ability to access another computer system from a terminal on the in-house system. This so-called terminal-to-computer interface may remain the most common type for the next several years.

The greatest potential appears to lie in the development of emulation-type interfaces, which use small front-end devices to accomplish the linkages among the systems. Such interfaces might be marketed by companies other than the turnkey vendors. No such interfaces were available in 1983, but at least two companies that have previously developed interfaces between bibliographic utilities and turnkey systems were seriously considering the introduction of such a product.

ACCEPTANCE OF TERMINALS BY LIBRARY PATRONS

There will be increasing emphasis on the development of user-friendly terminals for library patrons. The use of a terminal is perceived as a pleasant or unpleasant experience depending on the confidence felt by the user. The greater the amount of special command language that has to be learned and the greater the chance of making a mistake, the greater the discomfort of the user and the greater the resistance to a new technology. The problem will increase as libraries install more terminals in public areas for use by patrons.

Two aspects to this problem must be resolved: first, the elimination of the need for the user to know the correct system for entering a query—where the blanks belong, where the commas go and whether periods are needed after initials; second, the capability of providing inexperienced operators with a series of detailed instructions, while allowing more experienced users to bypass the instructions and get directly to the information they seek.

Mooers' Law remains one of the most important in library automation planning:

> An information retrieval system will tend not to be used whenever it is more
> painful and troublesome for a customer to have information than for him not
> to have it. A terminal is the computer to most users. Resistance to it means
> resistance to the system.[1]

Turnkey system vendors are usually reluctant to modify off-the-shelf terminals, but much of the improvement that might be made can be achieved by altering the appearance of the keyboard, displaying instructional graphics on the screen at the beginning of a procedure and modifying software. As one vendor observed in 1978, "Libraries don't specify what terminal features shall be offered so we do what appears to be the standard of the industry." This was substantially true in 1983, but CLSI, the largest vendor in the industry, was realizing a profit on a series of specialized terminals, especially touch terminals that eliminated keyboarding altogether.

Lack of attention by librarians to terminal features may contribute to user resistance when terminals are first made available to patrons. It is to be hoped that terminal design will become an important concern in future years.

RECORDS CONVERSION

A major breakthrough may still occur in records conversion. Kurzweil Computer Products, Inc. of Cambridge, MA, has marketed a second generation of its data entry machine that captures existing printed information and converts it into computer-readable form. The machine, which is built around a small minicomputer, reads any type font or combination of fonts whether typset, typewritten or photocopied.

The basic system stores a large file of character shapes that can be augmented with tables for special character forms unique to a particular application. The system's scanner matches what it sees against the file in the minicomputer memory and makes the identification of the character. It computes a confidence index measuring the reliability of each identification. The system will display for operator verification any character for which the reliability index is below a preset threshold. At each intervention the system displays not only its tentative identification but also a magnified image of the character as it appears on the document and several lines of surrounding text. The operator may correct the identification or confirm it, instructing the machine to continue. Corrections can be incorporated into the system's character definition tables for future use.

The system can convert up to 30 characters per second with a claimed error rate of one in 20,000 characters. Several of the $100,000 machines are in use for converting printed books into computer-readable form.

Considerable additional research would be required to convert library catalogs using such a unit, because red-ink subject headings, blue-ink location stamps and penciled holdings locations cannot be read by the present scanner. The small size of a catalog card also leads to inefficient operation of a scanner designed for full pages of text. The quality and variety of type on catalog cards is also less predictable than is the case for printed books. In the past, the company has been reluctant to commit the necessary resources to adapt the machine for library applications because of its preoccupation with what it considers to be more lucrative markets.

By the time the equipment is suitable for use in converting bibliographic records, the resource data bases in the bibliographic utility systems and the commercial bibliographic services may be so large that they will continue to offer the most attractive retrospective conversion method, because almost any library will achieve a hit rate of over 85% for monographs and serials. The optical scanning approach will still be useful, however, for converting records for documents, maps, audiovisual materials, microforms and other categories of materials not well represented in the resource data bases. The technology could also be used to convert community information files and special indexes.

AUTOMATING OFFICE PROCEDURES

When automation was introduced into libraries, it was first used for clerical and repetitive library tasks. With the growing emphasis on improving the inquiry features of circulation systems and providing online searching of bibliographic data bases, traditional office procedures have been overlooked. Many businesses and some libraries have already realized considerable improvements in office productivity by installing word processing equipment to speed typing and text editing.

There are many other office operations that readily lend themselves to automation. Among them are storage and retention of correspondence and unpublished reports, coordination of meetings and relaying of messages, preparation of budgets, and analysis of statistical data. While an integrated minicomputer-based library system could be used for these tasks, the best and least expensive software packages for all of these applications are written for micros. Within the next few years, many library administrative offices will be extensively automated. The administrator who plans wisely will seek compatibility between the office and library systems. Ideally the office micro(s) would be able to function as terminals to the library system, and records could be passed back and forth between the two systems.

The automation of the office will be relatively inexpensive compared with the automation of other parts of the library because development costs can be shared among tens of thousands of organizations of all types rather than a few hundred libraries.

REMOTE DATA BASE SEARCHING

Remote data bases will continue to play an important role in libraries. In the future, dedicated terminals will probably give way to universal terminals that can be used to access the local library system, a bibliographic utility and a remote data base offered by a data base broker or other organization.

Publicly available computerized data bases numbered more than 1600 as of June 1983, an increase of 1200 since 1979.[2] Some 400 of these files had emerged in the previous year. Only one online service, Dialog Information Services, Inc., offered access to more than 100 data bases, while most of the other nearly 200 services in North America and Europe offered only one data base.

An April 1982 study identified 950 data bases available through only one online service. Other data bases were very popular, however, being offered by as many as 28 online services. Thirty of the online services were European; they offered more than 230 data bases, two-thirds of which could be accessed only by dialing into a European host. There were 659 data bases that could be described as source data bases: files that provide the actual information sought, whether it be numerical, textual/numerical or full-text. Another 414 were reference data bases: files that point to publications, people, products or companies. One-third of the reference data bases were bibliographic and two-thirds were nonbibliographic. There were 60 data bases which were not clearly source or reference types. The number of nonbibliographic data bases is increasing faster than the number of bibliographic data bases.[3]

Bibliographic data bases are offered through brokers or data base services such as Dialog, Bibliographic Retrieval Services (BRS) and SDC Information Services. The largest full-text data bases, LEXIS and NEXIS, are offered through Mead Data Central. The largest online service specializing in nonbibliographic data bases is that offered by I.P. Sharp Associates of Toronto. The bibliographic services are already familiar to libraries, with more than 10,000 libraries making use of them. Libraries have barely begun to use the nonbibliographic data bases, but these are critically important because they provide information rather than pointers to information.

I.P. Sharp mounted its first nonbibliographic data base in 1973. In addition to offering access to data bases through its own international telecommunications network and Telex, I.P. Sharp also offers software to manipulate the data retrieved. Sharp's best known software package, MAGIC, facilitates the merging, cumulation, analysis, formatting and printing of data as required. Data drawn from Sharp data bases can be combined with data from other sources.

The Sharp pricing structure is different from that of most online services. The connect charge is only $1.00 per hour from any of 350 cities around the world, but there is a charge for computer utilization: CPU use, storage and data transfer off the Sharp system. These charges can be substantial if a great deal of data manipulation is undertaken on the system. The pricing policy reflects Sharp's history as a computer timesharing company.

The other comprehensive online service for nonbibliographic data bases is Data Resources Inc. (DRI), a company owned by McGraw-Hill Book Co. It has nearly 60 nonbibliographic data bases, which it produces or markets under license for other firms. DRI began in the late 1960s as an economics consulting firm. In addition to the data bases themselves, it offers software and consultation to facilitate the manipulation of the data, primarily for the preparation of economic forecasts. Recently, the company has begun to move toward full-text data bases. DRI's Datapro Research, the computer hardware/software report service, is among the first of these.

Users can subscribe to DRI for an annual fee or on a usage basis. The latter rate is higher, but does not require an upfront payment or a minimum annual usage. There is a separate pricing structure for data bases available through DRI but not produced by it. Access is primarily through value added networks such as Telenet, Tymnet and Uninet.

Emphasis is on U.S. and international data bases. The company claims unusual timeliness because it loads many of the data bases from the cities in which the data is gathered. DRI also claims to offer extensive online documentation of sources for all data. Keyword searching is available and may be applied across data bases.

VIDEO AND OPTICAL DIGITAL DISCS

As noted earlier in this chapter, the video disc and the optical digital disc offer great potential for library applications. One obvious use is for storage and distribution of bibliographic data.

It will take time for data base distributors to look beyond the video disc's entertainment applications to the medium's capacity for storing digital (machine-readable) information. Several manufacturers have already produced digitally encoded video discs, and others have developed optical digital discs, a closely related medium. These discs can store up to 10^{11} bits of information. The best way to conceptualize this capacity is to compare it with the storage capacity of the human brain, a book and some other common storage media. (See Table 8.1.)

Table 8.1 Video Disc as a Mass Storage Medium

Storage medium	Number of bits	Number of characters
Human brain	10^{15}	125 billion
Optical disc (single disc)	10^{11}	12.5 billion
Disk drive (IBM 3380)	2×10^{10}	2.5 billion
Book	2×10^{7}	2.5 million
Floppy disk	10^{7}	1.25 million

The rate of getting materials off a disc—the read rate—is quite good. Access rates being achieved in 1983 were typically 100 to 500 milliseconds (1 millisecond is one-thousandth of a second). NV Philips had already achieved 75 milliseconds. The error rate for reading information off discs is also quite acceptable. Philips and RCA are achieving 10^{-11} after correction. This is one error per disc. They are aiming for 10^{-12}, which would be only one error in 10 discs.

Neither video discs nor optical digital discs are erasable at this time. The former are stamped from a master, but the latter can be encoded and updated locally. The recommended approach is one of cross referencing updated information or writing a disabling code in a sector of obsolete data. The assumption is that the capacity is so high and the cost so low that the extra cost of engineering in erasability is not warranted. Nevertheless, some small firms are doing research into digital disc erasability.

The life of data on a video disc appears to be several decades and on a digital disc approximately 10 years. This compares with two to three years for information stored on magnetic tape. It is magnetic tape storage that is expected to be most affected by the new disc mass storage medium.

The implications for libraries go beyond the storage of large bibliographic files. The digital disc medium has the potential for storing the full text of journals and reference publications. While the technology may be mature enough for use in libraries by the mid-1980s, it may take another five years for the economic and attitudinal obstacles to be overcome. As discussed in Chapter 1, the diffusion rate of new technologies is slow in almost all applications, typically 10 to 15 years from development to widespread use.

The Library of Congress has already made a major commitment to video disc. Since 1981 the Cataloging Distribution Service (CDS) has been working with Xerox to set up a system for storing and reproducing digitized images of the 7.5 million LC cards not in machine-readable form. By the end of 1982 more than 150,000 images had been captured, and CDS made its first optical digital disc.

The system can actually enhance stained and worn originals after they are scanned by laser because an operator can change the contrast between the print and the background before the image goes onto a magnetic disc for storage. The optical digital discs are normally created when 200,000 or more images have been captured. It will be possible to display the images on high resolution (1024 lines) terminals or to print them on demand at high quality and speed. Because the system stores images, it it necessary to key in a record number to facilitate the later retrieval of the card images.

The success of this project (known as CARDS) encouraged the Library of Congress to award contracts for two additional projects, one to put films, slides and other visual materials on video discs, and the other to put images of pages of printed library materials on optical digital discs. The former project is similar to many video disc studies being undertaken by museums, art publishers, etc. Sony is the contractor for the $452,000 project. The latter is technically more challenging because optical digital disc technology is available only in prototype equipment. Teknekron of Berkeley, CA, is the contractor for the $1.7 million project. The company will attempt to assemble the system so that any one of several optical digital disc systems can be used, depending on the results of the various development programs now being undertaken by manufacturers.

The video discs will be mastered and replicated in multiple copies. The optical digital discs will be DRAW (direct read after write) and will be produced as single originals. Both projects were scheduled to be completed in late 1984.

VIDEOTEXT

Videotext (often called "videotex") is frequently used as the generic name for information retrieval via a modified home television set. In more precise usage, it refers to those systems in which the information is distributed from a computer data bank to the home TV over telephone lines or cable. In this sense, videotext is different from teletext, in which information is broadcast to the home using the blank space between the frames (the vertical blanking interval) of regular broadcast television images. Because they rely on wiring to deliver information, true videotext systems can operate in a two-way or interactive mode, allowing the user not only to receive information but also to transmit data back to the system. A large computer is used at the "head end" of the system so that many users can be served at one time. The decoder attached to the television receiver can accept data at a faster rate than a conventional television set and can also be used to formulate control signals to be sent back to the host computer.

Videotext systems can display diagrams and text in any of several sizes and in color. Once the text is displayed, it can be read like a book, and the viewer can "page" through the screens of data. Videotext can provide users with access to hundreds of thousands of pages of data. Teletext, on the other hand, offers limited information, because its capacity is, in effect, limited by the broadcast medium to the length of time a user is prepared to wait until the desired frame is broadcast sequentially.

In both videotext and teletext systems, the first thing the user sees is a contents page, which provides a rundown on the information available and directs the user to the subindexes for the various sections. From the subindex, the user is directed to specific pages of information. The modified television set has a small remote-control keypad (similar to that of a hand-held calculator) for controlling the system. In interactive videotext systems, that keypad can also be used to place orders, perform calculations or send other types of messages.

There were more than a hundred trials of videotext and teletext systems under way in the United States in early 1983, and some announcements of operational systems had been made. Several news media had contracted to provide news, and several retailers were planning to use videotext systems for advertising, with online ordering available to the viewer. The weather, stock market reports and sports results were among other information available. The information may be provided on the basis of the number of pages displayed or as part of a monthly subscription.

Libraries could become suppliers of information to videotext systems just as news services and retailers have. In Britain the charges for information storage in 1982 ranged from $2.50 to $8 per page annually, plus a service charge of $2000 to $8000, depending on the type of service offered.

There will obviously be copyright considerations in any such electronic use of published information by libraries. A publisher might insist that only it could legitimately distribute electronically what it has produced. Licensing or royalty payment agreements would probably have to be negotiated. For that reason, the most likely data bases for libraries to deliver initially would be their own catalogs and local files.

Not all commentators are sanguine about the long-term future of videotext, despite the fact that the technology represents a breakthrough in information retrieval and transaction processing. A study by International Resource Development, Inc. (IRD) of Norwalk, CT, argues that videotext is simply too unsophisticated for most business applications.[4] The trend may be toward integrated data processing/videotext/management computing systems. Several terminals that can display both videotext and computing formats are already being marketed.

IRD sees three sections in the videotext market: public service, private systems for businesses and closed user groups such as consortia or associations. Of the three, it posits that the last will probably prove to be the most durable, with private system sales never amounting to much and public service all but ceasing to exist by the end of the 1980s. IRD considers that preplanned national public services, such as the British Prestel system, now being widely tested in the United States are doomed to failure because they must try to be all things to all people, while the nature of videotext demands information tailored to the needs of specific target groups.*

ELECTRONIC MAIL SYSTEMS

In the first three years of the 1980s, over 600 libraries have begun using electronic mail—the fastest growing technology used in libraries. Electronic mail provides rapid transmission of messages between computer terminals. Users regard it as superior to regular postal and telephone services because:

• Unlike regular mail, electronic mail is instantaneous. A message can be composed, edited and transmitted in minutes.

• Unlike the telephone, electronic mail permits the transmission of messages irrespective of whether or not the recipient is immediately available. Surveys of office productivity show that only 25% of telephone calls succeed in coupling the right people on the first try. All electronic mail messages go to a central computer from which they can be accessed through any terminal in the system. Because the computer holds the messages until they are requested, there is no need for both parties to be available at the same time.

• Unlike most messages, a computer-recorded message cannot be misplaced. The system gives both the sender and receiver instant access to the message with proof of the times of transmission and pickup.

• It is possible to send the same message to several people with a single command.

Users of an electronic mail system generally proceed through the following steps:

• *Compose*: type a note, bibliographic citation or multipage document on the terminal.

• *Edit*: make changes in phrasing, add information and correct errors.

• *Send*: instruct the system to send the message to one or several designated persons.

• *Scan*: check the system to see if there are messages to be picked up.

• *Read/print*: read or print messages when there is time to deal with them.

• *Answer*: compose a reply and have it automatically addressed to the person from whom the initial message came.

---

*For further discussion of videotext technology and an assessment of its prospects, see Efrem Sigel, et al., *The Future of Videotext: Worldwide Prospects for Home/Office Electronic Information Services* (White Plains, NY: Knowledge Industry Publications, Inc., 1983).

Common library applications include communication among members of committees, intraorganizational communication among dispersed locations, reference query referrals from one library to another, announcements of meetings and transmission of interlibrary loan requests.

Several library groups have installed electronic mail systems. One of the largest efforts is that of the California Library Authority for Systems and Services (CLASS), which negotiated a group rate for use of the Tymnet, Inc. ONTYME Electronic Mail System. More than 400 libraries in the Pacific Northwest, Rocky Mountains and Plains States subscribe to the CLASS version of Tymnet's system, dubbed ONTYME-II.

In 1983 the standard rates for ONTYME-II included an annual subscription fee of $100 and a monthly maintenance charge of $10. Connect time costs varied from $2.85 to $5.75 per hour. There were also message and transmission charges. The rates were approximately 50% less than regular Tymnet charges. An average cost of $.50 per message was estimated by users. Alternative services were slightly more expensive; they included Telenet's Telemail, The Source and CompuServe. Microcom, a software firm, offers Microcourier, a software package that makes it possible for any Apple II micro user to call any comparably equipped Apple II.

Almost any general purpose computer terminal—either a CRT or printer terminal—can be used to access electronic mail services. A combination of a CRT and a printer is recommended. The following are essential characteristics of the terminal required for using ONTYME-II: ASCII (American Standard Code for Information Interchange) character transmission, asynchronous communication, and a 110, 300 or 1200 baud rate.

Libraries that use electronic mail are generally happy with the technology. In some interlibrary loan applications, its use has resulted in staff and equipment savings. Problems are sometimes encountered in low-message-volume situations where particular institutions or individuals have not established a regular "mailbox" clearing routine. In such cases, messages can languish uncollected for a week or more, undermining the whole rationale for this method of communication.*

TELEFACSIMILE

The new generation of telefacsimile equipment—digital machines that permit the transmission of a page of copy in less than a minute—has gradually begun to enter libraries. Digital facsimile is viewed in library applications primarily as a rapid and economical method of document delivery for middle range to long distance interlibrary loan transactions.

However, this technology is being harnessed in an innovative local application in the

---

*For more information on electronic mail, see Stephen Connell and Ian A. Galbraith, *Electronic Mail: A Revolution in Business Communications* (White Plains, NY: Knowledge Industry Publications, Inc., 1982.)

Denver Public Library. Concerned to maintain the level of reference service in branch libraries in the face of depleted staff resources, Denver Public has installed Rapicom, Inc. 6300 digital telefacsimile equipment in the central library and Rapicom 800s in 17 of its branch libraries. The machines transmit a page of information in from 15 to 45 seconds. The network allows fast delivery of requested materials from the central site to the branch libraries.

In providing the rapid delivery service, Denver Public supplies the first three pages of copy gratis and levies a $.50 per page charge on subsequent pages of information. Since the system began operation in late 1982, a number of users have opted to pay the copy charge rather than travel downtown to consult the material free of charge.

That telefacsimile is undergoing a renaissance is evident from the sales figures—while only 255,000 machines had been installed in North America by the end of 1980, 80,000 units were delivered in 1982. This growth can be expected to continue as the 15 or so companies now in the market expand their product lines and are joined by new competitors.

The spread of this technology to libraries may be hampered by memories of the limited success of slower (four to six minutes per page), older generation analog equipment of the 1960s. In assessing the appropriateness of digital telefacsimile in a particular institution or network, the library manager should:

• Establish a time standard of no more than 60 seconds for the transmission of a typical journal page. A machine that operates at a slower speed will result in unacceptably high telecommunications charges.

• Specify *digital* telefacsimile equipment. Not all subminute telefacsimile equipment is digital. However, digital machines combine the advantages of rapid transmission with superior resolution capabilities. While such capabilities are not critical in the transmission of regular print pages, they are essential when complex charts and copies of older published material are being sent. The typeset letters in older materials are often quite close together and this, together with the discoloration and shrinkage in paper that occurs over time, can make an image transmitted on lower resolution analog equipment unreadable.

• Specify equipment that meets the Consultative Committee on International Telephone and Telegraph (CCITT) Group III standard. Adherence to this standard will usually insure compatibility among the digital machines of different manufacturers. If a library also wishes its digital machine to be compatible with analog equipment, it should specify downward compatibility to Group I and/or II machines.

• Investigate the possibility of leasing or renting the equipment rather than purchasing it outright. The telefacsimile market is undergoing rapid change. Even though most of the digital machines have been introduced only since 1979, a fourth generation of equipment is under development. The new machines are expected to be capable of faster transmission with greater resolution than now available. The new generation machines will call for satellite, microwave or coaxial cable transmission. Development of standards for such machines has not yet been completed.

Further, a number of photocopier manufacturers are experimenting with the introduction of copying machines with telefacsimile capability. The machines could be used for conventional copying when not in use for telefacsimile transmission. In early 1983, Nippon Electric Co. introduced a new machine that it described as a telefacsimile machine but that could also be used as a copier, a computer printer, a Telex receiving machine and an electronic mail receiving machine. Its $12,000 cost—twice the average for telefacsimile machines—has limited sales, however.

TELECOMMUNICATIONS

In the near term, libraries will have to continue to rely on local telephone companies and cable television companies for local data communication and on value added networks (VANs) such as Tymnet and Telenet for long-distance communications. Two other telecommunications technologies are receiving considerable attention as potential competitors: satellite and fiber optics.

Satellite transmission is now being used in conjunction with cable for teleconferencing and distribution of video programming. The outlook for satellite use by libraries appears to be limited, however. "The cost-competitive position of satellites will not improve by 1995, and so satellites will remain economically viable...only for very long distance links," says Malcolm H. Ross in a 1982 study done by Arthur D. Little International (ADL) for the European Space Agency.[5] No major reductions in satellite costs can be expected because of the relative maturity of the existing space system technology. At present satellite communication is used for distances greater than 500 miles. In the future it may be limited to transcontinental and transoceanic data transfer.

Fiber optics is the technology of producing glass or plastic (optical) cables through which light can pass for long distances with only a slight loss of intensity. A laser is used as the light-producing medium. It is possible to transmit much more information in the form of light than as electrons through conventional copper or coaxial cables of comparable diameter. The carefully documented ADL study argues that fiber optic systems will become increasingly cost-competitive in the 1980s as production experience and economies of scale reduce costs.

Fiber optic cables are already beginning to appear in short high-capacity communications situations. Microwave, now usually used for high-traffic communications over distances of 25 to 500 miles, is also expected to be affected by the growth of fiber optic systems. The availability of competing data communication technologies should reduce prices over the long term—10 or more years. A major factor in any price reductions will be the continuation of a recent pattern of industry deregulation.

THE AUTOMATED LIBRARY IN 1990

The majority of libraries in 1990 will be automated, but they will not be paperless libraries. Acquisitions decisions will be based on extensive management information about library users and patterns of collection use, ordering will be online, and funds accounting will be done automatically. Shared cataloging will be a by-product of shared bibliographic data bases mounted on bibliographic utility systems or distributed on video disc or optical digital disc.

Online patron access catalog and circulation control functions will be commonplace because they have the greatest potential value for users. The user will be able to access both the holdings and current availability status of materials in an entire library system from a terminal in any library location or from the home or office using a computer terminal or a television receiver adapted for videotext. Automation will also have extended to the library office.

Libraries will continue to have collections of printed books and journals, but a significant percentage of statistical and directory data will be accessed through computer terminals, as will almost all bibliographic data. A librarian will have to be skilled in both printed and electronic media to serve patrons well.

Libraries will face commercial competition on all fronts, from electronic systems such as videotext to information brokers who respond to telephone queries for a fee. Most people will probably use several suppliers to satisfy their information needs. They will make their choices based on ease of use, speed of response and cost to the user. Libraries may remain the least costly to the user, but they may find it difficult to compete in ease of use or speed of response unless librarians become highly effective managers of technology.

FOOTNOTES

1. C.N. Mooers, "Mooers' Law on Why Some Retrieval Systems Are Used and Others Are Not," *American Documentation*, Vol. 11, 1960, p. 204.

2. *Directory of Online Data Bases*, Volume 4, Number 3 (Santa Monica, CA: Cuadra Associates, Inc., Spring 1983), p. 5.

3. Unpublished study done by Carlos Cuadra; information presented during a panel discussion at Special Library Association meeting, New Orleans, June 6, 1983.

4. Confidential unpublished multiclient study, 1983.

5. Consulting report in conjunction with the ADL study of ARTEMIS (Automatic Retrieval of Text from Europe's Multinational Information Service).

Appendix A: Selected Sources for Automated Products and Services

TURNKEY MULTIFUNCTION SYSTEMS

Avatar Systems, Inc.
11325 Seven Locks Rd., Suite 205
Potomac, MD 20854
(301) 983-8900

CL Systems, Inc. (CLSI)
81 Norwood Ave.
Newtonville, MA 02160
(617) 965-6310

CTI Library Systems, Inc.
120 E. 300 North
Provo, UT 84601
(800) 453-1195
(801) 373-0344 in Utah

DataPhase Systems, Inc.
3770 Broadway
Kansas City, MO 64111
(816) 931-7927

Data Research Associates, Inc.
9270 Olive Blvd.
St. Louis, MO 63132-0888
(800) 325-0888
(314) 432-1100 in Missouri

Easy Data Systems, Ltd.*
401-1200 Lonsdale Ave.
North Vancouver, British Columbia, Canada
  V7M 3H6
(604) 986-8261

Gaylord Brothers, Inc.
Box 61
Syracuse, NY 13201
(800) 488-6160
(315) 457-5070

Geac Computers (Geac Canada Ltd.)
6300 Variel Ave., Suite A
Woodland Hills, CA 91367
(213) 887-3180
or
309 Seaside Ave., Suite 304
Milford, CT 06460
(203) 877-1486

Sigma Data Computer Corp.*
5515 Security La., Suite 1100
Rockville, MD 20852
(301) 984-3636

Systems Control, Inc.
1801 Page Mill Rd.
Palo Alto, CA 94304
(415) 494-1165

Universal Library Systems, Ltd.
1571 Bellevue Ave.
West Vancouver, British Columbia, Canada
  V7V 1A5
(604) 926-7421

*Easy Data and Sigma Data offer packages custom-tailored to the requirements of the customer, unlike the table-driven "off-the-shelf" systems of true turnkey vendors.

INTEGRATED SOFTWARE PACKAGES

DOBIS/Leuven
IBM Corp.
10401 Fernwood Rd.
Bethesda, MD 20034
(301) 897-2059

NOTIS
Northwestern University
1935 Sheridan Rd.
Evanston, IL 60201
(312) 492-7640

VTLS
Virginia Tech Library Automation Project
113 Burruss Hall
Blacksburg, VA 24601
(703) 961-5847

ACQUISITIONS

Baker and Taylor Co.
6 Kirby Ave.
Somerville, NJ 08876
(201) 526-8000

Brodart, Inc.
500 Arch St.
Williamsport, PA 17701
(800) 233-8467
(717) 326-2461 in Pennsylvania

CATALOGING

Online Computer Library Center, Inc. (OCLC)
6565 Frantz Rd.
Dublin, OH 43017
(614) 764-6000

Research Libraries Information Network
 (RLIN)
Jordan Quadrangle
Stanford, CA 94305
(415) 328-0920

University of Toronto Library Automation
 Systems (UTLAS)
80 Bloor St. W., Second Floor
Toronto, Ontario, Canada M5S 2V1
(416) 923-0890

Washington Library Network (WLN)
Washington State Library
AJ-11
Olympia, WA 98504
(206) 459-6518

SERIALS

Few of the turnkey vendors had developed full serial control capabilities by mid-1983. However, OCLC and several subscription agencies offered online support, and several vendors were marketing stand-alone serial control systems.

Boley International Subscription Agency
310 E. Shore Rd.
Great Neck, NY 11023
(516) 466-5394
(212) 895-7282

California Library Authority for Systems and
 Services (CLASS)
1415 Koll Circle, Suite 101
San Jose, CA 95112-4698
(408) 289-1756

Ebsco Industries, Inc.
Subscription Services
P.O. Box 1943
Birmingham, AL 35201
(205) 991-6600

F.W. Faxon Company, Inc.
15 Southwest Park
Westwood, MA 02090
(617) 329-3350

Innovative Interfaces, Inc.
2131 University Ave., #334
Berkeley, CA 94704
(415) 540-0880

Meta Micro Library Systems, Inc.
311 W. Laurel, Suite 211
San Antonio, TX 78212
(512) 224-8455

ONLINE SEARCHING SERVICES

Bibliographic Retrieval Services, Inc. (BRS)
1200 Rte. 7
Latham, NY 12110
(518) 783-1161

Dialog Information Services, Inc.
3460 Hillview Ave.
Palo Alto, CA 94304
(800) 227-1927
(800) 982-5838 in California

System Development Corp. (SDC)
2500 Colorado Ave.
Santa Monica, CA 90406
(800) 421-7229

RECORDS CONVERSION SERVICES

Amigos Bibliographic Council
11300 North Central Expressway, Suite 321
Dallas, TX 75243
(214) 750-6130

Auto-Graphics, Inc.
751 Monterey Pass Rd.
Monterey Park, CA 91754
(213) 269-9451

Blackwell North America, Inc. (BNA)
6024 SW Jean Rd., Bldg. G
Lake Oswego, OR 97034
(503) 684-1140

Brodart, Inc.
500 Arch St.
Williamsport, PA 17701
(800) 233-8467
(717) 326-2461

Carrollton Press, Inc.
1911 N. Fort Myer Dr.
Arlington, VA 22209
(800) 368-3008

The Computer Company
1905 Westmoreland St.
Richmond, VA 23230
(804) 358-2171

Electronic Keyboarding Inc. (EKI)
140 Weldon Parkway
Maryland Heights, MO 63043
(800) 325-4984

General Research Corp. (GRC)
5383 Hollister Ave.
Santa Barbara, CA 93111
(805) 964-7724

Informatics, Inc.
6011 Executive Blvd.
Rockville, MD 20852
(301) 770-3000

Inforonics, Inc.
550 Newton Ave.
Littleton, MA 01460
(617) 486-8976

Library Systems & Services, Inc.
1395 Piccard Dr., Suite 100
Rockville, MD 20850
(800) 638-8725
(301) 258-0200

Science Press
300 W. Chestnut St.
Ephrata, PA 17522
(717) 733-7981

Also networks such as OCLC, RLIN, UTLAS, WLN (see Cataloging).

CONSULTANTS

Aaron Cohen & Associates
RFD #1
Box 636, Teatown Rd.
Croton-on-Hudson, NY 10520
(914) 271-8170

Joseph Becker
Becker and Hayes, Inc.
2800 Olympic Blvd., #103
Santa Monica, CA 90404
(213) 829-6866

Larry Berul
Berul Associates, Ltd.
5010 Nicholson La., Suite I
Rockville, MD 20852
(301) 984-9400

Richard W. Boss
Information Systems Consultants Inc.
P.O. Box 34504
Bethesda, MD 20817
(301) 299-6606

Cibbarelli & Associates
11684 Ventura Blvd., Suite 295
Studio City, CA 91604
(213) 760-8110

Computer Horizons, Inc.
1050 Kings Highway, N.
Cherry Hill, NJ 08034
(609) 779-0911

Carlos Cuadra
Cuadra Associates, Inc.
2001 Wilshire Blvd., Suite 305
Santa Monica, CA 90403
(213) 829-9972

Hank Epstein
Information Transform, Inc.
502 Leonard St.
Madison, WI 53711
(608) 255-4800

Susan Baerg Epstein
Susan Baerg Epstein, Ltd.
1992 Lemnos Dr.
Costa Mesa, CA 92626
(714) 754-1559

Maurice J. Freedman
100 W. 80th St. #85A
New York, NY 10024
(212) 496-8080

Lewis A. Gordon
Great Lakes Industries, Inc.
Box 801
Elgin, IL 60120
(312) 695-1455

Saul Herner
Herner and Co.
1700 N. Moore St., Suite 700
Arlington, VA 22209
(703) 558-8200

Justan Enterprises
Bonnie Juergens
Hugh Standifer
P.O. Box 33160
Austin, TX 78764
(512) 288-2072

Brigitte L. Kenney
Infocon, Inc.
400 Plateau Parkway
Golden, CO 80401
(303) 278-7411

Donald King
King Research Inc.
6000 Executive Blvd.
Rockville, MD 20852
(301) 881-6766

Mary A. Madden
Information America
1372 Peachtree St., NE, Suite 312
Atlanta, GA 30309
(404) 892-1800

S. Michael Malinconico, Associate Director
Technical & Computer Services
New York Public Library
The Branch Libraries
455 5th Ave.
New York, NY 10016
(212) 340-0811

Joseph R. Matthews
Joseph R. Matthews & Associates
213 Hill St.
Grass Valley, CA 95945
(916) 272-8743

Rob McGee
RMG Consultants, Inc.
P.O. Box 5488
Chicago, IL 60680
(312) 321-0432

Judy McQueen
Information Systems Consultants, Inc.
P.O. Box 34504
Bethesda, MD 20817
(301) 299-6606

Belden Menkus
Box 85
Middleville, NJ 07855
(201) 383-3928

Richard Meyer, Associate Director
Robert Muldrow Cooper Library
Clemson University
Clemson, SC 29631
(803) 656-3026

Lynda W. Moulton
Comstow Information Services
302 Boxboro Rd.
Stow, MA 01775
(617) 897-7163

Sandra K. Paul
SKP Associates
160 5th Ave.
New York, NY 10010
(212) 675-7804

Vincent K. Roach
Data Sciences, Inc.
125 W. Market St.
Indianapolis, IN 46204
(317) 632-3916

G. Susan Savage
Savage Information Services
608 Silver Spur Rd., #310
Rolling Hills Estates, CA 90274
(213) 377-5032

Ralph M. Shoffner
Ringgold Management Systems
Box 368
Beaverton, OR 97075
(503) 645-3502

Appendix B: Glossary

The following brief definitions are offered for laymen and may lack the precision a specialist might prefer. Only those terms used in this book and those most commonly used in the vendors' general literature are included.

AACR: See *Anglo-American Cataloging Rules.*

Access time: The time interval between the request to a computer for data and the instant response begins to be delivered. Also called *Response time.*

Address: The location in the storage of a computer of a name, number or other data element.

Alphanumeric: A character system consisting of both letters and numbers.

AM: See *Amplitude modulation.*

American National Standards Institute (ANSI): A body that has established voluntary industry standards for business equipment manufacturers. It has accepted many programming languages as ANSI standards, which can be taken as evidence that they are well established and generally sound. ANSI standard languages used in automated library systems include COBOL, FORTRAN and MUMPS.

Amplitude modulation (AM): Modulation in which data are transmitted by varying the amplitude (height) of the carrier wave. One amplitude is selected to represent a "1" bit and another to represent a "0" bit.

Analog: The representation of values or characters electronically by means of physical variables (variations of electronic pulses). Voice-grade telephone lines are analog, as distinguished from the digital representation used in computer systems.

Analog signal: A signal that is formed by a continuous range of amplitudes or frequencies, for example, a continuously varying current or the human voice. Contrast with *Digital signal*.

Anglo-American Cataloging Rules (ACCR): A widely accepted set of rules for describing and establishing name headings for books and other library materials. The second edition (AACR 2) was published in 1978.

ANSI: See *American National Standards Institute*.

APL (A Programming Language): A high-level programming language that uses unique characters to represent functions to be performed; APL is well suited for interactive problem solving.

Applications package: A set of computer programs or software used to solve problems in a particular application.

Applications program: A single program, or sequence of instructions, written to solve a specific problem facing organizational management.

ASCII: American Standard Code for Information Interchange, a standard code that assigns specific bit patterns to each letter, number and symbol.

Assembler program: The translator program for an assembly language.

Assembly language: A programming language similar to machine language but made up of convenient abbreviations rather than groupings of 0s and 1s. It is referred to as an intermediate-level language between lower-level machine language and higher-level programming languages such as COBOL or FORTRAN.

Asynchronous communication: A method of data transmission dependent only on the condition of the transmitting line at that time and not on the condition of the hardware or software at either end.

Authority file: A record of the correct headings to be used for names, subjects or series. Its purpose is to provide consistency.

Auxiliary storage: See *Secondary storage*.

Background: The execution of lower priority programs at the same time as higher priority ones but without interfering with them. The alternative is to process lower priority work overnight.

Backup: Alternate procedures, equipment or systems used in case the original is destroyed or unavailable.

Bar-coded labels: Machine-readable identification symbols printed on paper strips for attachment to library materials and patron identification cards. Bar code symbols represent binary numbers by using height, width, distance between vertical bars or relationship among bars to express characters. Codabar labels, developed by Pitney Bowes and marketed by Monarch, are the most widely used in library applications.

Batch processing: Processing of data after they have been accumulated over a period of time as opposed to doing it immediately or online.

Baud: A unit of signaling speed. One baud most commonly means that one bit moves through a line every second. Common low and high speed baud rates are 300 bits per second (bps) and 1200 bps.

Bit: A unit of information that is the smallest unit in the binary system used in computer systems. A bit is a representation of one or zero. The combination of bits represents the data of interest to libraries.

Bit-mapping: A method by which the electronic signals on a video screen are controlled. Each position on the screen is represented by a "bit" in a two-dimensional matrix. A "1" bit indicates that the screen should be "on" at this location; a "0" bit indicates the screen should be "off" at the position.

Block size: The number of logical data elements included in one physical record, usually on a medium such as magnetic tape or magnetic disk.

Buffer: An area used to hold data during transfer from one device to another, e.g., from the CPU to a terminal or from the disk to a line printer.

Buffer device: A device that provides temporary storage. It is used to balance unequal operating speeds of different devices.

Bug: A malfunction or error.

Bus: A pathway used to transmit signals from a source to a destination.

Byte: A series of bits that constitute a unit, most commonly eight bits.

Cache memory: An intermediate storage area or buffer between the CPU and main memory. Cache memory increases computer system performance by eliminating the need to access main memory for data stored in the cache memory.

CAM: See *Content addressable memory.*

Card punch: A device to record information in cards by punching holes in them.

Card reader: A device that senses the holes in a punched card and translates these into machine code for the computer.

Carrier: On an analog transmission medium, electrical current that can be modulated to carry data.

Cathode ray tube (CRT): An electron tube in which electrons strike a phosphor-coated screen to form an image. Used as a means of input and output to a computer. Also known as a video display unit (VDU).

CBX: See *Computerized private branch exchange.*

CCD: See *Charge coupled device.*

Central processing unit (CPU): The part of the computer that actually performs the computations.

Channel: Any physical path over which signals may be transmitted.

Charge coupled device (CCD): A memory device in which stored data circulate rather than staying in one fixed location.

Chip: A small slice of silicon containing one or more electronic circuits. A typical computer contains hundreds of chips.

Circuit switching: A channel allocation technique in which connection is made to the destination prior to the start of the message transmission. Message routing is completed before the message is sent.

Coaxial cable: Cable consisting of one conductor placed concentrically within an outer conductor of larger diameter.

Collateral archive: Historical data that can be collected and retrieved online.

Command: An instruction in machine language such as from a terminal to the computer to execute a particular program.

Compiler: A computer program used to translate other computer programs (in a high-level language) into machine language.

Composite terminal: A terminal that offers light pen or OCR wand and keyboard functions in one unit.

Computerized private branch exchange (CBX): An exchange established by the communications common carrier for transmission of digitized messages, including digitized voice.

Content addressable memory (CAM): A storage device in which storage locations are identified by their contents rather than by addresses. Data are retrieved from a memory cell when their content matches the content of the data at the input.

Contention: A technique of controlling a data communications channel in which the device sends an electrical signal in order to seize the channel when needed.

Controller: Any device in a computer system that supervises a function; for example, a communications controller. It may be a function of the CPU or of a smaller secondary processor.

Conversion: The process of changing from one method of recording and manipulating data to another, e.g., from manual to computerized or from one computerized system to another.

Core memory: Main memory made of iron cores, which could be magnetized in either of two directions. These memories are quickly being replaced by memories using semiconductors.

CPU: See *Central processing unit.*

CRT: See *Cathode ray tube.*

Cursor: A solid underscore that appears under a character or space on a CRT or VDU to show where the next character entered will appear.

Data base: The entire collection of files maintained in the computer system.

Data communications: Electronic transmission of encoded data from one location to another.

Data compression: The reduction of storage space used by eliminating gaps or redundancies not essential to an intelligible record.

Data management: The organizing, locating, storing, maintaining and recovering of data and the programs developed to accomplish that.

Data processing: A sequence of operations that manipulates data according to a previously developed plan.

Data set: See *Modem.*

Debug: To identify, locate, analyze and correct a malfunction or error in a computer program.

Decoder: Device for reversing a coding process; e.g., demodulation in a modem.

Dedicated computer: A computer devoted to exclusive use as opposed to one that is shared with other users who maintain different files and may control them differently.

Diagnostic routine: A program that is run periodically to detect malfunctions or errors.

Digital signal: A signal that is formed by discrete electrical pulses using a two-state or binary system. Contrast with *Analog signal.*

Direct access: Any method of accessing data in which the time necessary for accessing the data is independent of the storage location. Also known as random access.

Direct view storage tube (DVST): A graphics terminal in which the image does not have to be continuously refreshed because the phosphorescent material used on the screen emits energy slowly.

Disk: The principal means of storing information in a computer system. The capacity of disk storage is usually measured in megabytes.

Disk drive: A direct access device that is used to read or record data on a magnetic disk.

Disk pack: A package containing several individual platters, commonly five or more, each of which has hundreds of tracks of information. The tracks are subdivided into several dozen sectors. It is these sectors that are "accessed" when entering or reading information.

Distributed processing system: An in-library system that does not stand alone, but relies on a host computer outside the library to do part of the processing. The host usually has a greater storage capacity and faster printing capability.

Documentation: The detailed record of decisions made in developing a computerized system; this record is necessary to replicate, repair or enhance the system.

Downtime: The time during which a system or a part thereof is not functioning.

Dumb terminal: A terminal that can do input/output but no data processing.

Dump: To copy from storage, or the actual data from that action. A tape dump is often obtained for backup or for sending to another library.

DVST: See *Direct view storage tube.*

EBCDIC: A standard code that assigns specific bit patterns to each letter, number and symbol. EBCDIC stands for Extended Binary-Coded Decimal Interchange Code and is used on IBM-type computers.

Erasable programmable read-only memory (EPROM): Programmable read-only memory that can be erased and reused.

Facsimile: A method of transmitting paper documents, pictures, etc. by a telecommunications channel. The document is scanned at the transmitter and reconstructed at the receiver. Also called FAX.

Failsafe: A procedure by which the computer can store certain data from its own main memory when it detects that it is failing, e.g., through a loss of power . This facilitates rapid restart when power is restored or stabilized.

FAX: See *Facsimile*.

Fiber optics: Cables composed of glass fibers that carry data via pulses of a laser beam.

Field: A part of a record. The specific area used for a particular category of data such as title or call number.

File layout: The arrangements of the elements of the file, including the order and size of the elements.

Filtering: The removal of "noise" signals during the process of imaging.

Firmware: "Halfway" between hardware (the machine) and software (programs written in a programming language). Firmware consists of programs (instructions and/or data) that are implemented in read-only memory (ROM) or memory that is programmable in a less flexible manner than writing in a programming language, e.g., programmable read-only memory (PROM) or erasable programmable read-only memory (EPROM).

Fixed-length record: A record that has the length fixed in advance rather than being varied according to the actual extent of the contents. Contrast with *Variable-length record*.

Flip-flop: A circuit capable of assuming either of two stable states.

Frequency division multiplexing: A technique whereby total bandwidth of a communications channel is divided into smaller bands that can transmit different signals simultaneously. Each device sharing the channel is assigned to a given subchannel.

Frequency shift keying: Modulation of the frequency of a carrier signal by a digital modulating signal. The frequency of the carrier is raised by a specified amount to represent a "1" bit and lowered by a specified amount to represent the "0" bit.

Front-end systems: A form of distributed processing. The library uses a computer, usually a micro, for only minor processing, and the bulk of the work and the files are handled on a host computer.

Full-duplex channel: A channel that transmits data in both directions simultaneously. This is accomplished by the use of four separate transmission paths.

Function: A specific machine action that may be initiated by a function key or by an internal instruction. A number of predefined functions can be initiated by a terminal operator.

Gate: An integrated circuit that produces an output only when certain specified conditions are present.

Gate array: Integrated circuits consisting of a series of gates that the manufacturer can link together to perform any function desired by the customer.

Half-duplex channel: A channel that transmits data in both directions but not simultaneously.

Hard copy: A printed copy of machine output as opposed to temporary display on a CRT or VDU.

Hardware: All of the tangible components of the computer system, including the central processing unit, disk drives, terminals, etc., as distinguished from the programs that operate the system.

Hit: A successful matching of two items. In data conversion, one may seek to utilize another library's records by search key to minimize the time and cost of data entry. The hit rate is the percentage of successful matches.

Hologram: An image recorded by causing interference between a laser reference beam and a beam reflected from the object. Three-dimensional images are possible. Holograms can be used for data storage and have the advantage that extremely high recording densities can be achieved.

Host computer: The controlling or principal computer in a system that ties two or more computers together.

Housekeeping: Operations that prepare or maintain the computer to do the processing needed.

Imaging: The transformation of video signals into a digital form of storage.

Index or index search: An index is used to locate the contents of a file as well as the pointers to access the data. In an index search, the system matches the search key with an index entry that points to the physical location. If a file is very large, there will be several levels of indexes. The index entries are arranged sequentially; therefore it is possible to search by partial keys when one does not have full author or title.

Injection logic: A method by which electronic charges are stored in a memory cell. This type of storage is referred to as charge injection transistor memory (CITM).

In print: Currently available from the publisher.

Input/output (I/O): Refers to the insertion of data or instructions into a computer or the transfer of processed data from the computer to the user. Examples of input/output media are punched cards, cathode ray tubes and printers.

Inquiry: A request for information from storage.

Integrated chip: Thin wafers of silicon on which integrated circuits are built.

Integrated circuit: An entire circuit, including active and passive components, built on a chip. Integrated circuits offer small size and high reliability, low cost and high speed.

Intelligent terminal: A terminal with its own internal logic circuitry; this allows some functions, such as editing for syntax errors or reformatting, to be done at the terminal rather than at the CPU. A lesser grade of "intelligence" is a terminal with storage capability (its own buffer) but not the logic necessary for higher level processing.

Interactive computer graphics: The use of a computer terminal for drawing lines and images.

Interface: The linking of two or more computers. A computer-to-computer interface links the CPUs directly. A terminal-to-computer interface links a terminal of one system to the CPU of another.

International Standard Book Number (ISBN): A distinctive and unique number assigned to a book. It is hoped that eventually the ISBN system will be used by all publishers throughout the world.

International Standard Serial Number (ISSN): A distinctive and unique number assigned to a serial.

Interrupt: Temporary suspension of a sequence of operations.

Inverted file: A file created from another by altering the sequence of the fields or creating a cross index to another file so that a key word identifies a record. Call number access often involves inverting a file.

I/O: See *Input/output*.

ISBN: See *International Standard Book Number*.

ISSN: See *International Standard Serial Number*.

Jobber: A wholesaler who stocks or supplies the books of many publishers for resale to bookstores and libraries.

K: See *Kilobyte.*

KB: See *Kilobyte.*

Keyboard: A device for entering data by pressing keys as opposed to badge reading or scanning with a light pen or OCR wand.

Keypunch: A keyboard device that punches holes in cards to represent data so that they will be machine-readable.

Kilobyte (K or KB): 1024 bytes; usually used to describe the primary storage capacity of a computer. See also *Megabyte.*

Language: A set of software representations and rules used to convey information to the computer.

Language processor: A computer program that compiles, assembles or translates a specific programming language into a form the computer can operate on.

Large-scale integration (LSI): Fabrication of circuits with a large number of transistors on a single chip.

Light pen: The pen-shaped device used to read bar-coded labels.

Line printer: A device that prints all of the characters of a line as a unit, as contrasted with printing one character at a time.

Machine language: A programming language that enters instructions into a computer in a form that the computer does not have to translate or interpret in order to use.

Magnetic bubble memory: Very high capacity chips that use small cylindrical magnetic domains ("bubbles") that move over the surface of a magnetic film. The presence of a bubble corresponds to a "1" bit and the absence of a bubble to a "0" bit.

Magnetic disk: A flat circular plate with a magnetic surface on which machine-readable data can be stored by magnetization of parts of the surface.

Magnetic tape: A tape with a magnetic surface on which machine-readable data can be stored.

Mainframe: A full-sized computer system based on a CPU, the capacity of which is usually measured in megabytes. Normally used to describe large computers of the type operated by a municipality, academic institution or other parent organization.

Main memory (also known as main storage): Storage that can be directly accessed as opposed to auxiliary storage or secondary storage such as that on magnetic tape. See also *Storage.*

Maintenance: Any activity to keep computer hardware or software running, including not only repairs, but also tests, adjustments and scheduled replacements.

Management information: Data organized in such a way as to aid in the management of an enterprise. It usually consists of statistical cumulations.

MARC: MAchine Readable Cataloging, a program of the Library of Congress in which machine-readable cataloging is distributed in LC format.

MB: See *Megabyte*.

Megabyte (MB): One million bytes, a term normally used to describe the secondary storage capacity of a computer such as disks.

Memory: See *Storage*.

Memory controller: A device that regulates the reading of data from or to the main memory of a computer system.

Microprocessor or microcomputer: A complete computer processor on a single integrated circuit chip approximately the size of a dime.

Microsecond: One-millionth of a second.

Millisecond: One-thousandth of a second.

Minicomputer: A physically compact digital device that has a central processing unit, at least one input/output device and a primary storage capacity of at least 64,000 characters (64K).

Modem: For modulator-demodulator, a device that makes computer signals compatible with communications facilities. Modulation encodes the original signal for the communications medium. Demodulation decodes it. Also called a data set.

Multidrop channel: A single communications line shared by several devices. One end of the line is connected to a communications controller. The line may be used by only one device at a time.

Multiplexor: A device used in data communications that permits several devices to share a single transmission line.

Network: A number of communication lines connecting a computer with remote terminals or with other computers.

OCR: Optical character recognition, or a type font that can be read by both humans and machines. The best known is OCR-A, the type approved by the National Retail Merchants

Association. An OCR wand is a device that, when passed over the special type font, "reads" the data into the machine.

Offline: Equipment or storage not under control of the central processing unit.

Online: Equipment or storage under the control of the central processing unit so that a user can interact directly with the computer.

Parallel transmission: Data transmission in which individual bits of a character or word are transmitted over adjacent data channels and assembled at the receiving end. Contrast with *Serial transmission.*

Password: A symbol that a user must give when first beginning to use a computer system to identify him/her or to provide access to restricted functions.

Peripheral equipment: Any physical part of a computer system, other than the central processing unit, that provides the system with external communication.

Pointer: An address or other way of indicating location.

Polling: A technique by which each of the terminals or computers sharing a communications line is queried to get information.

Port: That part of the central processing unit that provides a channel for receiving or sending data from or to a remote device. More than one such device may be put on a port.

Printer: An output device that converts machine code into readable impressions on paper or microform.

Program: A series of instructions for computer actions to perform a task or series of tasks.

Programmable read-only memory (PROM): Memory that cannot be erased— accidentally or intentionally; used for systems or basic applications programs rather than for data.

Prompting or prompts: A function that tells a terminal user what to do next or asks what he or she wants to do next.

Queue: A waiting line of data, either in the order received or in some other previously determined order.

RAM: See *Random access memory.*

Random access memory (RAM): Storage technique in which the time required to retrieve data is independent of location. Random access memory can be read from and written into by the user.

Raster scan: A graphics terminal that uses a dot representation for each character. Characters are maintained by a scanning electron beam which refreshes the image at least 20 times per second.

Read: To transfer data from an input device or an auxiliary storage device to a computer.

Read-only memory (ROM): A storage technique in which instructions or data in memory can be accessed but not altered by the user. Used to store interpreters, monitors, etc.

Real-time processing: The provision of data at the time a user is at a terminal so that those responses may be used in further queries.

Record: A collection of related items of data treated as a unit. The author, title and call number fields may constitute the item record in a circulation system.

Recording density: The number of bits per inch or the number of bits per cubic inch that can be stored on any storage medium.

Record length: A measure of the size of a record, usually in characters.

Register: A high-speed memory used for arithmetic and logical operations, address indexing, linking subroutines and, in some cases, as a program counter.

Release: A periodic revision of software that is distributed to all customers of a turnkey system vendor.

Resist: A photographic-type emulsion, sensitive to ultraviolet light, that is used as a coating in the production of integrated chips.

Response time: The time between the entry of a query and the beginning of the response on the screen, printer or other output device. Same as *Access time*.

ROM: See *Read-only memory*.

Search: To examine a number of items in order to find one or more that meet specified characteristics or properties.

Search key: The data entered in for the conducting of a search.

Secondary storage: Storage outside the CPU using tape, magnetic disks or another medium.

Semiconductor: A material which has low resistance in one direction and high resistance in the opposite direction. This difference in resistance makes possible the use of semiconductors for computer logic circuits and memory.

Sequential search: The examination of each item in the order in which the items are arranged on the disk or other storage medium. The method is most suitable for such records as patron names and addresses.

Serial transmission: Data transmission in which individual bits of a character or word are transmitted one after the other over the same channel. Contrast with *Parallel transmission.*

Shared logic: A situation in which a controller supplies the logic and uses dumb or intelligent terminals to access the central computing facility.

Simplex channel: A channel that transmits data in one direction only.

Simulate: To represent features of the behavior of one system by another, such as using a large computer to simulate the behavior of a minicomputer for the purpose of testing software or the effect of a specific number of terminals.

Software: A set of programs, procedures and documentation concerned with the operation of a computer system.

Stand-alone: A computer system that is capable of performing all the specified functions without the help of another computer, as opposed to a distributed processing system.

Standing order: An order for all works in a series, all volumes of a set or all editions of a work.

Static memory: Memory that retains its values in the event of power failure. Also termed "nonvolatile" memory. Volatile memory loses its values in the event of a power failure.

Storage: The memory of a computer. The device in which data are held for later retrieval and use. See also *Main memory, Secondary storage.*

Store-and-forward switching: A channel allocation technique in which the whole message is transmitted to the next node and stored there in a queue until the proper outgoing circuit is available, then transmitted to the next node.

Streaming: A process by which data are written on magnetic tape, interjecting inter-record gaps after each data block is written without starting and stopping the tape drive between blocks of data.

Synchronous transmission: A method of data transmission wherein blocks of characters are sent in a continuous stream without each character being framed between start and stop bits. An internal clocking mechanism within the modem is required to synchronize sender and receiver. Contrast with *Asynchronous transmission.*

Teleprocessing monitors: Programs that manage telecommunications traffic over a network of communications channels.

Terminal: A point in the computer system at which data can be entered or withdrawn. The most common terminals are CRTs and printers.

Throughput: The total amount of work a computer system performs in a specified time period.

Time-division multiplexing: A technique in which two or more signals are sent on the same channel using different time intervals.

Time sharing: A method of using a computer system that allows a number of users to execute programs at the same time, with the system servicing them in such rapid sequence that the users appear to be handled simultaneously.

Transfer time: The amount of time required to transmit data from one storage device to another storage or display device.

Transistor: A semiconductor with three electrodes. The current between one pair of electrodes is a function of the current between the other pair. Transistors are used for switching or amplification of a signal.

Truncate: To terminate a process or to shorten fields according to previously established rules.

Turnkey system: A complete system provided by a vendor, including equipment, software, installation and training.

Update: To modify a file with current information.

Utility programs: Programs, often supplied by the hardware manufacturer, for executing standard operations such as sorting, merging, reformatting data, renaming files and comparing files.

Variable-length record: A file in which the records need not be uniform in length but are only as long as the amount of data warrants.

VDU (video display unit): See *Cathode ray tube*.

Very large-scale integration (VLSI): Fabrication of circuits with a very large number of transistors on a single chip. With this technique, circuits containing more than 35,000 transistors have been made.

Video disc: A disc on which optical images may be stored. Video discs are often written and read using laser beams.

Virtual memory: Space on secondary storage devices that appears to the computer user as main storage. The instructions and data required by a program are divided into segments and only the necessary segments are brought into main memory at any one time.

VLSI: See *Very large-scale integration.*

Volatile: Becoming erased or destroyed when power is cut off. Contrast with *Static memory.*

Winchester disk: Large-capacity, high-density magnetic disk with sealed head-to-disk assembly that is nonremovable. These disks are highly reliable.

Write: To transfer data from a computer to an output device or to auxiliary storage devices.

Bibliography

Alternative Catalog Newsletter, all issues.

Anderson, Carol Lee, and Jo Ellen Herstand. "Automating a Library: An Investigative Study." 1979 (ERIC Document Reproduction No. ED 191 496).

Automated Acquisitions. Washington, DC: Association of Research Libraries, Office of Management Studies, 1978 (SPEC Kit 44).

"Automated Acquisitions: What's Good? What's Bad? What's Missing?" (Phonodisc recorded at ALA's 97th Annual Conference, Chicago, June, 1978.) Chicago: American Library Association, 1978.

Avedon, Don M. *Computer Output Microfilm*, 2nd ed. N.M.A. Reference Series, no. 4. Silver Spring, MD: National Microfilm Association, 1971.

Aveney, Brian, and Mary Fischer Ghikas. "Reactions Measured: 600 Users Meet the COM Catalog." *American Libraries* 10 (February 1979): 82-83.

Axford, H. William, ed. *Proceedings of the LARC Institute on Acquisitions Systems and Subsystems*. Tempe, AZ: LARC Association, 1973.

Bahr, Alice Harrison. *Automated Library Circulation Systems 1979-80*, 2nd ed. White Plains, NY: Knowledge Industry Publications, Inc., 1979.

— — —. *Microforms: The Librarian's View, 1978-79*. White Plains, NY: Knowledge Industry Publications, Inc., 1978.

Barkalow, Pat. "Conversion of Files for Circulation Control." *Journal of Library Automation* 12 (September 1979): 209-213.

Barley, Kathryn S., and James R. Driscoll. "A Survey of Data-Base Management Systems for Microcomputers." *Byte* (November 1981): 208.

Bernstein, Judith, ed. *Turnkey Automated Circulation Systems: Aids to Libraries in the Marketplace*. Chicago: American Library Association, Library Administration and Management Association (LAMA), 1980.

Berst, Jesse. "10 Pitfalls to Avoid in Buying a Small Computer System." *Interactive Computing* (May/June 1981): 4-9.

Bierman, Keneth John. *Alternatives to Card Catalogs for Large Libraries: The Current State of Planning and Implementation*. Final Report to the Council on Library Resources Fellowship Project, June 1975. Washington, DC: Council on Library Resources, 1975.

Bolef, Doris. "Computer-Output Microfilm." *Special Libraries* 65 (April 1974): 169-175.

Boss, Richard W. *Automating Library Acquisitions: Issues and Outlook*. White Plains, NY: Knowledge Industry Publications, Inc., 1982.

— — —. "Circulation Systems: The Options." *Library Technology Reports* 15 (January/February 1979): 7-105.

— — —. "General Trends in Implementation of Automated Circulation Systems." *Journal of Library Automation* 12 (September 1979): 198-202.

— — —. *The Library Manager's Guide to Automation*. White Plains, NY: Knowledge Industry Publications, Inc., 1979.

Brownrigg, Edward B., and J. Michael Bruer. "Automated Turn-key Systems in the Library: Prospects and Perils." *Library Trends* 24 (April 1976): 727-36.

Bruer, J. Michael. "The Public Relations Component of Circulation System Implementation." *Journal of Library Automation* 12 (September 1979): 214-218.

Buckland, Lawrence F., James Dolby, and Mary Madden. *Survey of Automated Library Systems; Phase I*. Final Report. Maynard, MA: Inforonics, Inc., 1973.

Butler, Brett. "The Conversion of Manual Catalogs to Collection Data Bases." *Library Technology Reports*, 14:2 (March/April 1978).

C.A.C.U.L. (Canadian Association of College and University Libraries). "Workshop on Library Automation, University of British Columbia, Vancouver, April 10-12, 1967." *Automation in Libraries*. Ottawa, Canada: Canadian Library Association, 1967. (ERIC Document Reproduction No. ED 021 583.)

Carter, Ruth, and Scott Bruntjen. *Data Conversion*. White Plains, NY: Knowledge Industry Publications, Inc., 1983.

Cravey, Randall, et al. *Computer Output Microfilm (COM): An Alternative to Card Catalogs for SOLINET Members*. Atlanta, GA: Southeastern Library Network, Inc., February 1977.

Data Communications Testing, Training Manual. Palo Alto, CA: Hewlett-Packard Co., 1980.

DeGennaro, Richard. "Library Automation: Changing Patterns and New Directions." *Library Journal* 101 (January 1, 1976): 175-183.

Divilbiss, J.L., ed. *Negotiating for Computer Services: Proceedings of the 1977 Clinic on Library Applications of Data Processing.* Urbana, IL: University of Illinois Graduate School of Library Science, 1978. (ERIC Document Reproduction No. ED 167 078.)

Dranov, Paula. *Microfilm: The Librarian's View.* White Plains, NY: Knowledge Industry Publications, Inc., 1976.

Dunlap, Connie R. "Mechanization of Acquisitions Processes." *Advances in Librarianship*, Vol. 1. Melvin John Voight, ed. New York: Academic Press, Inc., 1970, pp. 35-57.

Essentials of Data Communication. Beaverton, OR: Tektronix, Inc., 1979.

Fayen, Emily Gallup. *The Online Catalog: Improving Public Access to Library Materials.* White Plains, NY: Knowledge Industry Publications, Inc., 1983.

Feher, Kamilo. *Digital Communication, Facilities, Networks and System Design.* New York: John Wiley & Sons, Inc., 1978.

Ford, Stephen. *Acquisitions of Library Materials*, rev. ed. Chicago: American Library Association, 1978.

Fosdick, Howard. "The Microcomputer Revolution." *Library Journal* 105 (July 1980): 1467-1472.

Fundamentals of Computer Output Microfilm. Silver Spring, MD: National Microfilm Association, 1974.

Gaddy, Dale. *A Microfilm Handbook.* Silver Spring, MD: National Microfilm Association, 1975.

Gorman, Michael. "Toward Bibliographic Control: Short Can Be Beautiful." *American Libraries* 10 (November 1979): 607-608.

Greenberg, Esther. *Innovative Designs for Acquisitions and Cataloging Departments as a Result of Library Automation.* Cleveland, OH: Case Western Reserve University School of Library Science, 1974. (ERIC Document Reproduction No. ED 096 993.)

Grosch, Audrey N. *Minicomputers in Libraries, 1981-82: The Era of Distributed Systems.* White Plains, NY: Knowledge Industry Publications, Inc., 1982.

Harris, Virginia B., Katherine Frohmberg, and William A. Moffett. *Research on the Impact of a Computerized Circulation System on the Performance of a Large College Library.* Oberlin, OH: Oberlin College, 1979. (NTIS Report. PB80-137938.)

Hawken, William R. *Evaluating Microfiche Readers: A Handbook for Librarians.* Washington, DC: Council on Library Resources, 1975.

Hayes, Robert M., and Joseph Becker. *Handbook of Data Processing for Libraries.* New York: John Wiley & Sons, Inc., 1970.

Housley, T. *Data Communications and Teleprocessing Systems.* Englewood Cliffs, NJ: Prentice-Hall, Inc., 1979.

Hull, Philip, and S. Porter. "Use of COM and OCR in the Guelph Cataloging Systems." *The LARC Reports* (Computerized Cataloging Systems Series) 1 (1974): 95-103.

"Implementation of Automated Circulation Systems." 2 cassettes. Chicago: American Library Association, 1978. (From Library Adminstration Division Annual Conference program. Order No. 78/17.)

Juergens, Bonnie. "Staff Training Aspects of Circulation System Implementation." *Journal of Library Automation* 12 (September 1979): 203-208.

Kamilo, F. *Digital Communication*. Englewood Cliffs, NJ: Prentice-Hall, Inc., 1981.

Kearney, J.M., and J.S. Mitutuinovich. *A Guide to Successful Computer System Selection*. Park Ridge, IL: Data Processing Management Association, 1976.

Kennedy, James H., and James S. Sokoloski. "Man-machine Considerations of an Operational On-Line University Library Acquisitions System." *The Information Conscious Society: Proceedings of the 33rd ASIS Annual Meeting*, Vol. 7. Washington, DC: American Society for Information Science, 1970. (Available from Knowledge Industry Publications, Inc., White Plains, NY.)

Kenney, Brigitte L., ed. *Cable for Information Delivery: A Guide for Librarians, Educators and Cable Professionals*. White Plains, NY: Knowledge Industry Publications, Inc., 1984.

Kimber, Richard T. *Automation in Libraries*, 2nd. ed. Elmsford, NY: Pergamon Press, 1974.

King Research, Inc. *Alternatives for Future Library Catalogs: A Cost Model*. Rockville, MD: King Research, Inc., 1980.

Kozumplik, W.A. "Computerized Microfilm Catalog." *Special Libraries* 57 (September 1966): 524.

Kuo, F., ed. *Protocols and Techniques for Data Communication Networks*. Englewood Cliffs, NJ: Prentice-Hall, Inc., 1981.

Lancaster, F. Wilfrid, ed. *Applications of Minicomputers to Library and Related Problems: Proceedings of the 1972 Clinic of Library Applications of Data Processing*. Urbana, IL: University of Illinois Graduate School of Library Science, 1974.

— — —. *Problems and Failures in Library Automation: Proceedings of the 1978 Clinic on Library Applications of Data Processing*. Urbana, IL: University of Illinois Graduate School of Library Science, 1979. (ERIC Document Reproduction No. ED 174 223.)

Library Automation, Introduction to Data Processing. White Plains, NY: International Business Machines Corp. Data Processing Division, 1972.

Madden, Mary A. "Minicomputer Applications in Acquisitions and Cataloging." *Information Politics: Proceedings of the 39th ASIS Annual Meeting*, Vol. 13. Washington, DC: American Society for Information Science, 1976. (Available from Knowledge Industry Publications, Inc., White Plains, NY.)

Malinconico, Michael S. "The Economics of Output Media." *Proceedings of the 1976 Clinic on Library Applications of Data Processing*. Urbana, IL: University of Illinois Graduate School of Library Science, 1977.

——— and Paul Fasana. *The Future of the Catalog: The Library's Choices*. White Plains, NY: Knowledge Industry Publications, Inc., 1979.

Martin, Susan K., and Brett Butler, eds. *Library Automation: The State of the Art II. Papers presented at the Preconference Institute on Library Automation*. Chicago: American Library Association, 1975.

Matthews, Joseph R. *Choosing an Automated Library System: A Planning Guide*. Chicago: American Library Association, 1980.

McAllister, Shirley A., and Helen A. Gordon. *Online Terminal/Microcomputer Guide and Directory 1982-83*. Weston, CT: Online, Inc., 1982.

Meyer, Richard W., and John F. Knapp. "COM Catalog Based on OCLC Records." *Journal of Library Automation* 8 (December 1975): 312-321.

Nelson, Bonnie R. "Implementation of On-line Circulation at New York University." *Journal of Library Automation* 12 (September 1979): 219-232.

"New Technology" (column in *Library Journal*). Features short articles on new products and services for libraries.

Palmer, Richard. "Library Automation: Getting What You Pay For." *Innovative Developments in Information Systems: Their Benefits and Costs: Proceedings of the 36th ASIS Annual Meeting*, Vol. 10. Washington, DC: American Society for Information Science, 1973. (Available from Knowledge Industry Publications, Inc., White Plains, NY.)

Palmer, Richard P. *Case Studies in Library Computer Systems*. Ann Arbor, MI: R.R. Bowker, 1973.

Pearson, Karl M., Jr. "Minicomputers in the Library." *Innovative Developments in Information Systems: Their Benefits and Costs: Proceedings of the 36th ASIS Annual Meeting*, Vol. 10. Washington, DC: American Society for Information Science, 1973. (Available from Knowledge Industry Publications, Inc., White Plains, NY.)

Pierce, A.R. *Circulation and Finding System*. Blacksburg, VA: Virginia Polytechnic Institute and State University, 1979. (ERIC Document Reproduction No. ED 183 141.)

Pope, Nolan F. "Networking via Automated Circulation Systems: Problems and Potentials." *Bulletin of the American Society for Information Science* 5 (June 1979): 27-29.

Rendler, Richard E. "SCICON Comes to San Jose." *Library Journal* 106 (February 1, 1981): 311-313.

Robinson, F. "The Uses of OCR and COM Information Work." *Program* 8 (July 1974): 137-148.

Rockman, Ilene F. "The Potential of On-Line Circulation Systems as Public Catalogs: An Introduction." *RQ* 20 (Fall 1980): 39-58.

Roden, M.S. *Analog and Digital Communication Systems*. Englewood Cliffs, NJ: Prentice-Hall, Inc., 1979.

Rogers, Kenneth A. "Cost Benefits of Computer Output Microfilm Library Catalogs." *Innovative Development in Information Systems: Their Benefits and Costs: Proceedings of the 36th ASIS Annual Meeting,* Vol. 10. Washington, DC: American Society for Information Science, 1973. (Available from Knowledge Industry Publications, Inc., White Plains, NY.)

Saffady, William. *Computer-Output Microfilm: Its Library Applications*. Chicago: American Library Association, 1978.

Salmon, Stephen R. *Library Automation Systems*. New York: Marcel Dekker, Inc., 1975.

Salton, Gerard. *Dynamic Information and Library Processing*. Englewood Cliffs, NJ: Prentice-Hall, Inc., 1975.

Savage, N. "LAMA Spotlights Pitfalls in Automated Circulation." *Library Journal* 105 (August 1980): 1570.

Schultheiss, Louis A. " Data Processing Aids in Acquisitions Work." *Library Resources and Technical Services* 9 (Winter 1965): 66-72.

Schwartz, Philip J. *COM: Decisions and Applications in a Small University Library*. Menomonie, WI: Wisconsin University, 1976.

Shammugan, K.S., *Digital and Analog Communication Systems*. New York: John Wiley & Sons, Inc., 1979.

Survey of Vendors of Automated Circulation Systems—System Interfaces. Washington, DC: Metropolitan Washington Library Council, Metropolitan Washington Council of Governments, 1979 (Report No. 79-102.)

Swanson, Don R. "Requirements Study for Future Catalogs." *Library Quarterly* 42 (July 1972): 302-315.

Taylor, Gerry M., James W. Hansard, and James F. Anderson. "Cut to Fit." *Library Resources and Technical Services* 14 (Winter 1970): 31-35.

Tedd, L.A. *Introduction to Computer-Based Library Systems*. London: Heyden & Son, Inc., 1977.

Thomas, Sara M., and Lester P. Needle. "Applications of COM (Computer Output on Microform) in the Library Systems." *Microform Review* 4 (April 1976): 95-96.

Ungerleider, S.L. "A Study of COM Usability in the Technical Processing Area of Yale University Library." *Journal of Micrographics* 7 (November 1973): 81-89.

University of Rochester Library Task Force on Access Systems. *Report*. Rochester, NY: University of Rochester Library, 1980.

Veaner, Allen B. "Major Decision Points in Library Automation." *College and Research Libraries* 31 (September 1970): 299-312.

Viterbi, Andrew J., and Jim K. Omura. *Principles of Digital Communication and Coding*. New York: McGraw-Hill Book Company, 1979.

Weber, David C. "Personnel Aspects of Library Automation." *Journal of Library Automation* 4 (March 1971): 27-37.

Wood, Richard J. *The IBM System 7 On-Line Circulation System at Slippery Rock State College*. Slippery Rock, PA: Slippery Rock State College, 1980. (ERIC Document Reproduction No. ED 190 095.)

Index

ABOUT THE AUTHOR

Richard W. Boss is Senior Management Consultant, Information Systems Consultants Inc., Bethesda, MD, and Boston, MA. He has served as a consultant to more than 100 libraries and library consortia on the selection and procurement of automated library systems. In addition, he has been a consultant to vendors of automated systems.

Mr. Boss was formerly University Librarian at Princeton and Director of Libraries at the University of Tennessee at Knoxville. He is the author of *The Library Manager's Guide to Automation* (1979) and *Automating Library Acquisitions: Issues and Outlook* (1982) in Knowledge Industry Publications' Professional Librarian series. His many other publications include "Automated Circulation Systems," *Library Technology Reports* (May/ June 1982); *Developing Microform Reading Facilities* (Microform Review, 1981); and "Automation and Approval Plans," *Advances in Understanding Approval and Gathering Plans in Academic Libraries* (Western Michigan University, 1970). He is a graduate of the University of Utah and holds an M.A. in Library Science from the University of Washington.

WITHDRAWAL